AVAILABLE LIGHT

AVAILABLE LIGHT

RECOLLECTIONS
&
REFLECTIONS
OF A SON

BY REAMY JANSEN

H \s

HAMILTON STONE EDITIONS

Library of Congress Cataloging-in-Publication Data

Jansen, Reamy
 Available light: recollections & reflections of a son/ by Reamy
Jansen.
  p. cm.
 ISBN 978-0-9801786-0-9 (alk. paper)
    1. Jansen, Reamy—Family. 2. Mothers and sons—United States. 3.
    Fathers and sons—United States. I. Title.
    II. Title: Available light, recollections and reflections of a son.
    PS3610.A587Z46 2010
    814'.6–dc22
    [B]

2009008528

Cover by Lou Robinson

H \s

HAMILTON STONE EDITIONS
P.O. Box 43, Maplewood, New Jersey 07040

ACKNOWLEDGMENTS

Literary Magazines: Thanks go to the following journals and their editors who have previously published some of these essays: *Alimentum, The Literature of Food; Bloomsbury Review of Books; Enskyment.org; Evansviille Review; Fugue; Higginsville Reader; MM Review; Oasis; Talking River Review; UnpleasantEventSchedule.com.*

Residencies and Awards: Thanks also to The Corporation of Yaddo, The Geraldine R. Dodge Foundation, The Jerome Foundation, New Millennium Writing, The Office of the Chancellor/The State University of New York, The New York Mills Arts and Cultural Center, Virginia Center for the Creative Arts, Gell House: Writers & Books.

People: And many, many thanks to John Allman, Suzanne Cleary, Barbara Hoffert, Neal Kreitzer, Cynthia MacDonald, Dan and Janet Masterson, Gardner McFall, David Means, Daniel Nester, Rochelle Ratner, Anson Rabinbach, Gabriel Stone-Jansen, Paul Stone-Jansen, Neal Storrs, Art Winslow, Linda Wolfe. Special thanks to Elizabeth Stone who showed me so much about words, to my always supportive editor at the *Bloomsbury Review of Books*, Marilyn Auer, and to my wife, Leslie Grover Jansen, who read all this, again and again, with a loving and critical eye and so helped in letting this little book go off on its own.

In memory of my parents
Arthur Jansen and Betty Culbertson Jansen

&

to two boys
Paul and Gabriel
—now men
hardy filaments always

TABLE OF CONTENTS

Introduction: A Word of Beginning /11

I

Openings /17
Interiors /21
Carefully Taught /28
Arsenic /48
How I Became a Sensitive Soul/53

II

Available Light: Notes on Going Blind /61
Slowness /72
Household Gods /74

III

Acorns /84
Dogwoods /91

IV

"Taste This"–A Eulogy /94
Pears /97
Last Words /100

AVAILABLE LIGHT

A WORD OF BEGINNING

"I have made a virtue of my casual ways."
—Czeslaw Milosz

At age eight or so I buried my Lone Ranger code ring in a Maxwell House tin in our back yard. I had no code to put in it, not that I can remember, other than my name. But I liked the idea of buried treasure, something squirreled away, later unearthed. However, I did such a fine job of digging deeply, both hands grasping and struggling with the haft of my dad's shovel, and then covering the place with leaves and twigs that I couldn't find it again, ever, no matter how often I returned. This first failed effort didn't stop me from attempting others, such as burying my mad uncle's sharp-shooting medals. Again, I might as well have thrown them out the window of my parents' Chrysler. That's often the way it is with me and things—first saved, later lost.

My carelessness with family artifacts in my possession hasn't improved much. I never lose them outright, but I can't always locate them—my mother's Willkie campaign buttons; an 8 x 10 photo of my grandfather, Adolph, sitting before his hot-type machine in the press room of *The New York Sun*; the family trees my father wrote up of both sides of the family

Jansens, Reinholds, Stuarts, and Culbertons; a few of my father's four-hund-red-plus transportation articles from *Barron's* ("Tortuous Progress," "More Dead Weight"), and my mother's books: *Black Majesty*, Sholem Asch's *East River*, Anatole France's *Penguin Island*, and Paul DeKruif's *Microbe Hunters*. If I eventually find something, it's because I've stumbled upon it.

Everything is unintentionally broadcast about my hundred-year-old house. There is no box or label right for any of it. Again, in childhood, I did attempt to put some things into a container. I had selected a box the size of a microwave; one covered in slick, white paper, where I cut something along the lines of a mailbox slot in the lid. I then took any number of family photos out of their albums and put them into the box by way of the slot, around which I had written in glue—My Family Photos—and had then sprinkled with red and blue glitter. When I displayed the box to my mother, the images had already started to curl and roll up like rhododendron leaves in winter. I can't remember if we ever restored them to their original places.

If I had the beginnings of ideas about things, the ideas would have to go forth without their objects being ordered. Still, I can't help periodically pondering the reuniting of my diaspora of little things. Some part of my day is generally spent in imagining, if not realizing, the perfect box, both finite and limitless.

In a bit of serendipity, however, assembling a rush of family items presented to me was what led to my first essay, "Household Gods." The essay recounts the story of my father's decision to sell the family home, the one I grew up in, and move to my sister's (he'd been a widower of some twenty years). I did much of his packing, assisted by my two young sons, Paul and Gabriel. Over a time of what may have been close to two months, my dad supplied me — "perhaps the boys would like this" — with the things that are now incoherently dispersed throughout the cellar of my home in the Hudson Valley.

For not the first time I knew what it meant to feel displaced and insufficiently buoyed by things, and I began to compose "Household Gods" almost immediately after my father was transplanted to Connecticut. The satisfying process of composing this essay taught me that I would best be able to assemble a cabinet of curiosities in my mind and on the page. I knew that I was likely to be a writer of essays and that those compositions short and long would be the way I would reclaim my father, whose portrait and its back-lighted glow look down from the top of the bookshelf onto my side of the bed, the book case holding volumes of Goethe and Schiller that my great-uncle Otto, who lived singly in a cold-water flat in Jersey City, bound in beautiful leather he hand-tooled.

I have no portraits of my mother, although I have tried to paint her in some places here—at times with the slashing smears de Kooning might have recognized as his but might mainly recall the pensive distraction of Eakins' portrait of Miss Van Buren. I think I've fairly caught her features, the complex, distracted, and often flinching self, and that I've done her some justice here, too.

I, of course, am present throughout *Available Light* as an "I," the alloy: *sonfather*. I had my first boy at the same age that my father became father to me, and my second son arrived in the same number of years—three and a half—that it took for my sister to succeed me.

I wrote the essays that make up *Available Light*, almost all about three generations of fathers and sons, over a period of eight years, during summers when I wasn't teaching essays or commenting on them in the fall and spring semesters at my college. The collection feels whole and entire. And it feels finished. Sufficient.

Nevertheless, being a father is how I found my bearings as a man, and so the subject will be ever with me as a compass point, and it has almost reflexively surfaced in other essays and poems I have written. Even when I was a visiting writer in Germany, writing about Baden-Württemberg, Thuringia, and Bavaria, the suburbs of Long Island, fathers and sons, my youth and middle age arrived to keep me company wherever I was in the German Palatine. In fact, I even visited, in Bavaria, the same Bayreuth opera house my father had sixty years before me. I'd like to believe I sat in his seat or, better, perhaps the one next to it.

I

And I cannot but often wonder to see fathers, who love their sons very well, yet so order the matter, by a constant stiffness, and a mien of authority and distance to them all their lives, as if they were never to enjoy or have any comfort from those they love best in the world till they had lost them by being removed into another.

—John Locke, "Some Thoughts Concerning Education"

And afterward I saw other things. Always, afterward, one sees things.

—Marguerite Duras, "The Death of the Young British Pilot"

OPENINGS

Two things in our kitchen pantry marked the gates of adulthood and tolled both the beginning and ending of my childhood days. The first was the patterned blue revenue stamps, ribbons stretched tight, about to be broken, over the tops of my parents' yellow-labeled gin bottles, of whose contents all I then knew was the bright, liquid vapors of juniper. On a lower shelf, though, was the other—a row of big blue cans of Maxwell House Coffee, with the thick, white bell of a cup curving over the can's grooved metal surface, its image angled so that that remaining good-to-the-last, chocolate-hued drop was forever suspended, always about to fall. Well before my reading of Keats, this art provided me with my first sense of silent time and perhaps the prospect of watching and waiting.

As I was already curled in sleep in the early evening while the martinis were being made, mornings were another matter. Then, I would rise from my bed, awakened by the smell of coffee and go down into the unlighted kitchen. I would find the tableaux of my parents sitting across from one another in the sun's early beams at a small, yellow enameled table with just room enough for the two of them: my mother still in my father's robe of blue checks facing my suited father soon to depart.

I would watch them at their cups, talking above the misting brims, sometimes sweeping the dark, liquid surfaces out of the way like censers as a page of the newspaper was being folded. Such assured attitudes over coffee formed the axis on which turned the gnostic world of adults. Its hidden core seemed clasped within a hermetic blue cylinder, one giving off a reptile's guardian hiss when its seal was broken and whose inrush of air penetrated my nostrils with the fine scent of ground coffee. The opening of the can was a weekly ceremony my mother presided over later in the morning, while my small self stood in attendance. The can, she said, should not be touched by me, as it presented a world of bloody dangers to small boys. Nevertheless, these offices long remained ones I wished to perform.

Containers of this sort, on being opened, were meant to be resealed by metal tops formed by the stripping away of a band of metal girdling the can. A rudimentary key was soldered to its bottom and could be snapped off by levering it away with the fingers. (When my thumb and index finger finally became strong enough to do this, the cans had changed and their keys were gone, and soon after that my parents switched to "instant" in glass jars, claiming that this particular brew tasted just as good, and, even later, they no longer talked in the morning, my mother's distilled and troubled sleep leaching further and further into the day. And by then, after cold cereal and milk, I would head to school with the growing knowledge that adulthood was not really mastery, but might be, rather, aloneness.)

The prizing away of the key became the first step in a progress toward steaming coffee. Accomplished by an adult, this separation was a simple one. But it was as nothing to the threading of the metal tab at the top of the can through the slotted opening of the key. The little flap of metal needed to be bent away slightly to be mated with this device. Again, adult fingernails were required, along with motor skills surpassing mine. Even my mother's nails, bitten down as they were, seemed adequate to the task. The key then needed to be twisted away from the can's body, the handle carefully held parallel to the top, the rim guiding the key's course. This first twist, with the tab snapping the vacuum seal, inaugurated a sequence of others that had to be managed with steadiness and care, for the tab was attached to a belt of metal meant to be pulled away in even half turns.

What came forth was a gently increasing roll of bright, razor-sharp ribbon, so luminous as to seem freshly peeled from the can and which, my mother assured me when I asked for a try, would cut down into the flesh and expose the white bone of a child's finger, opening a spigot of blood, as if being given a full turn all its own. Her fingers and knuckles, sometimes offered in evidence, were inscribed with faint, white traceries of scar tissue and recently healed cuts.

If my mother's luck held, the roll would finally come to a halt and then be easily broken loose with a slight, but decisive, turn of the key. Things could go wrong along the way, however, if her concentration wavered and her wrist action became uncertain in its charting of the regular latitudes of the can's circumference. In such cases, the roll headed off on a rebellious, tapering longitudinal course, zooming out from its own center like a Chinese yo-yo, which droopily refused to return to its original mooring. If this wayward turn couldn't be righted, the thing wound up looking like a tangled watch spring, with the whole sharp-edged mess having to be pulled away with pliers.

Detached properly, though, a many-ringed roll of metal would break off, the key embedded in its center. This separate object could become a dangerous toy (recovered later from the garbage), a squatting little boy's top skating over the polished hardwoods of the living room, if the key was spun deftly enough. Of course, an adult couldn't be bothered by such childish things but, rather, would then set about the task of trying to lift the newly formed lid away from the can. This action was occasion for further damage, as the tips of the fingers became freshly endangered in pulling at the sharp, new top created by the absent strip of metal. And minor cuts would occasionally blossom at the ends of my mother's fingers, brought on with repeated openings and closings of the can, often the result of the lid becoming ill fitting and harder to replace after each morning's brewing for my father.

Her task completed, my mother would frequently remind me of the can's malevolent properties. It was one of several inductive particulars illustrating how the material world could strike without warning. I would listen every morning in the court of her kitchen, watching as she scooped the coffee out of the can and into the percolator, following her healing fingers down to the bottom to the last scattered grains.

INTERIORS

No one in this family touches. We maintain separate orbits, ones I monitor from a center that has been gradually weakening since early childhood. A disembodied eye, I take in everything from no particular vantage point.

Gray-haired, ruddy, cheerless, and quick to stretch his lips in disapproval, my father, on weekends during daylight, is a habitué of the margins of our property, maintaining the environs through not-overly-skilled mowing, random weeding, and desultory pruning. Still, the flora overgrows and looks uncared for, despite being tended to. Mountain laurels and white-flowered rhododendrons crowd the front walk. A bereft male holly tree presses too closely against the house, bruising its gray branches against the brown, shingled sides. Shrubs and trees combine to create a frayed, dark green belt, girdling the house.

Indoors, despite a preference for working in the corner, my father is pretty much at the center of the living room: his presence fills the large, well-proportioned rectangle that includes six full-sized windows, a deep, tiled brick fireplace, and French doors that open west onto a substantial, blue-gray, thickly-slated terrace. (My mother casts aspersions on the neighbors' lesser "porches" and often goes on to make invidious distinctions between our irregular, hand-hewn Cyprus shingles and the cheap, uniform pine that scales over the neighbors' houses)

By day, the living room's window shades, its flowered curtains, and rich, dark-red drapes smother the light. At night, though, the rough textures and deep colors of the drapes become more visible, and the room gives off a kind of red warmth. The walls offer dark, framed lithographs of the Pantheon, the cathedral at Rouen, and other architectural highlights of Western Civilization.

My favorite print, however, exhibits a less imposing subject matter, although it is the largest and murkiest among them. It hangs at the darkest end of the room, which lends mystery to what I already consider a fascinating pictorial narrative. It's a scene in winter, of a small, gothic-revival country church situated in a dusky, snow-covered landscape, the light weakly filtering through the tree tops' empty branches. A thin line of road banked by small drifts creates an off-center diagonal on which a couple clearly is on their way to a service, presumably evensong. The proximity of the destination conveys a kind of serenity, and I am frequently fixed somewhere within the aspect of its surface.

In contrast to the living room's comfortable appointments stands a folding card table, at which my father writes nightly. It is of the kind you often see magicians cover with a fringed and gaudy cloth, and it's hard to resist murmuring "presto" when all three legs snap simultaneously into place as the fourth is levered away from the underside. The table could be put away as soon as its temporary service is discharged, but its status is virtually permanent, given how most of its surface is covered, weighted with clippings from *The Wall Street Journal,* issues of *Railway Age,* or drafts of financial articles, along with all the detritus of writing—circular typewriter erasers, red pencils, desk scissors, a heavy, bronze ruler. Flanked by a ream of yellow scratch paper and a small pile of carbon-paper, layered like mica, sits a black enameled Remington portable that my father pounds like a clavier from which he hopes to produce more sound. Here, in this more-than-temporary stationing, he seems at home. His nimble, six-fingered typing resonates through the house, which trembles even more when he depresses the shift key, causing the heavy, cylindrical platen to rise, then, returning to its lower case setting, drop with a slight crash. He hammers steadily through much of the evening and often well into the night, while my mother, sitting in a nearby wing chair, drink ready to hand, occasionally ornaments his three-bar rests, his fingers tapping the air, with a comment on the day. His silent concentration is a wonder of its own.

My domain is the basement, a dimmer universe parallel to the house's extensive first floor. Here are the laundry room and coal cellar, along with a chamber holding a massive oil-burning furnace shrouded in thick white asbestos insulation; this engine periodically gives off a malevolent rumble that strikes shivers into me. The biggest room in the basement is known as the "play room," without, as far as I can tell, any ironic meaning. It lies immediately below, and has the same dimensions as, the living room. At least two thirds of its wall space is covered by a silver-gray sealant, topped by a band of chalky whitewash. A single light fixture, parsimonious with light, between two of the floor joists illuminates a large, threadbare oriental carpet whose visible pattern is only a dim recollection of the weaver's art. Other families in the area — ones with the porches and cheap shingles — are transforming their basements into "rec. rooms" with dropped ceilings, recessed lighting, floor tiles, imposing television consoles, and varieties of cozy, overstuffed seating. My lower realm never changes. Despite its appealing dimensions, the "play room" will remain musty and inhospitable.

Down here the stages of my childhood are demarcated by the objects I am given to play with, beginning with a set of solid, beautifully finished maple blocks. With them I build extensive towns, with bridges, roads, railroad tracks, freight yards, and a town hall. I pursue this civic project alone, even when I am visited with a baby sister. (My father comes down once, as I urge him to view my capital city, "Washingtown," spelled out in red crayon. Silent, pencil in hand, he bends down and flicks out the second "w" and returns to his typewriter above.)

In my early-teens I become a budding scientist, equipped with Bausch & Lomb microscope, an A.S. Gilbert chemistry set, and an assembly of make-shift rockets filled with a solid fuel that I create. Between the years of blocks and explosions come woodworking and model railroading. In the latter phase I am the lone engineer piloting a set of Lionel steam engines, coal tenders, and diesel switchers. A neighbor helps me set up my tracks on a pair of saw horses topped by plywood sheets. (My father, though, is especially good at getting people to show me how to do things, which I appreciate. I learn bait casting from one neighbor, fly-fishing from another, a fast ball and breaking pitches from yet a third, and I am always well equipped. Nevertheless, I usually participate in these activities alone, without teammates.)

Other fathers and sons create what seem to me contoured Hudson River School landscapes for their train sets, but my model railroad table remains relatively flat and spare, lifted from the Dust Bowl, although I have fashioned a lake from blue construction paper and an ungainly tunnel from bent coat hangers and shirt cardboards. For grass I dye pencil shavings. I keep hoping my father will come downstairs and join in, but it all looks so unappealing, even to me, that I don't blame him for his absence.

For a while, my trains run on a regular schedule, especially when my father is overhead percussively thumping out the latest developments in railroad securities. We are, in this way, playing together. (While I am at college, my mother gives these trains away, along with the big blocks of my early days. But my father, somehow intuiting my love of childhood things— and this surprises me—puts in hiding everything else, including a boxed set of large maple dominos, also made by A.S. Gilbert, that, later, my two sons and I will build small towns with.) In the last stage of childhood, the late teens, I move upstairs into the light. I become a musician, but remain no less isolated.

In the living room, my parents' separate book collections face each other from opposite walls. His favorites are all about railroading: histories of the Missouri Northwestern and the Union Pacific, or more general transportation reading, such as Van Meter's *Trains, Tracks, and Travel.* They are kept behind the glass doors of his mahogany secretary. I regularly take them out to explore their black and white past, where magnates and politicians are ferociously bearded, and the engines are massive, vibrant, threatening presences. Testing my ability to recognize nomenclature, I strive to recognize the 4-8-8-4 Type steam engines, which were "built and used only by Union Pacific," according to one book my father gave me. The world of railroading has the weighted substantiality of steel, an iron certainty of direction.

My mother sits in a big, chintz armchair, enveloped in a cone of yellow light, and she always seems to be reading volume after volume of the same book—*The Case of . . .* by Erle Stanley Gardner. Consuming a book a day, journeying late into the night through the pages, she avoids my father. The books my mother once read—those of Maupassant, Captain Marryat, Hugo and Poe—are at the other, more literary, end of the room. My mother is too active in her perpetual mysteries to be likely to go back to the nineteenth century and reread Maupassant's *Bel-Ami* or Hugo's *Ninety-Three.* Her collection of cheap paperbacks, however, is not to be found in the living room, where it would be on public display. With their tantalizingly lurid and déclassé covers, they are the sort of things one keeps out of sight, and she has piled them high in the maid's room. From whom or where my mother collects these volumes—possibly her secret connection to the common currency of isolated and lonely suburban housewives of the 1950s—is a mystery to me.

The rest of the time my mother is a creature of the kitchen, where she pads about in a housedress that's inexpensive enough to be a point of inverted pride. (Later, the dress will be unbelted to allow freedom for a swollen liver.) Coming and going in carpet slippers, she serves us our food with little talk, and over the years frozen foods come to crowd out our warm homemade meals. TV dinners become the ubiquitous entree, accompanied by Bird's Eye frozen vegetables, which, in a double-boiler, melt down like giant ice cubes. I can still recall the metallic scrape of silver utensils on aluminum trays, which were then carefully washed, stacked and put away for no clear purpose.

While I am still little, the medicine cabinet over her ancient and monstrously-legged, porcelain kitchen sink daily holds a small jelly glass of clear liquid, whose fluctuating levels are a barometer of her consumption, ebbing, then mysteriously rising, and, invisibly falling again, a cycle that regularly repeats itself throughout the morning and afternoon. When I ask what the stuff is, she tells me that it's cleaning fluid, poison.

When I return from school I enter through the kitchen door, since, as in most American homes, the front one is rarely used, and ours has already begun to abrade and decay. I pass through the faint illumination of the kitchen and traverse an even darker pantry to reach the darkest place of all, the bottom of the stairs. I stand beside a grandfather clock—one that has never worked—and lift my gaze. The darkly gleaming mahogany railing, curved as a wish, parallels the carpeted stairs and forms a diagonal to my line of sight, which spirals up to the second floor, whose bedrooms are joined by the polished arc of the balcony. My eyes' journey comes to a halt at the door of my parents' bedroom. At this time of day the door may either be closed or left open to the width of a small finger. In this room she will be taking her afternoon nap. In years past I would have attempted to wake her, but now I know that she needs to rest, and I have always accommodated her needs. One afternoon she was exotic in repose, stretched out naked as an odalisque on the *chaise longue* in that large and sunny room; in later years, she moved to the double bed.

As I look up the stairway I wonder if she is avoiding me or gathering energy so that later she can ignore my father and not have to accompany him to bed. Or is she doing both? No matter how long I stand in my shadowed niche, she will not wake for me. I go into the curtained and shaded living room and wait in my father's chair and rest.

CAREFULLY TAUGHT

in memory of Betty Baird Culbertson, 1904-1973

Pink at their center, darkly edged by what remained of her lipstick, her lips looked fresh cut. "Jews have moved in," she said, a pronouncement coming from the unlighted front hallway, her platform for afternoon commentaries. Returning from grade school, I had just entered through the kitchen. A current of outrage seemed to flow over her body, and, like static electricity supplied from one of our costly Oriental rugs, the charge leapt over to me. Momentarily, I was jolted, but that particular, invidious voltage never took hold fully.

She was listing slightly, her feet in slippers pushed out of shape from broken toes badly reset. An inexpensive housedress hung limp on her body, carriage frail in the upper arms and shoulders, while the torso, where once there had been a waist, slightly swelled by the dawning of liver damage. She had been waiting the afternoon for me, while I was finding the longest route home. Looking through the distracted and shifting planes of her face, I could tell that she believed that she would have an ally as she recounted the day's trials.

"Jews," in fact, were merely a single family whose pleasant, red brick house was located at the end of the block, an incursion limited to the corner. The transgression that had so animated her was that Mrs. Immer, a wife and the mother of two boys, was already trying to ingratiate herself with the neighborhood. (How did my mother know her name? I wondered. To ask, which I wasn't supposed to do, would be immediately linked to doubts about her veracity, and stability.) Mrs. Immer seemed to be acting as her own outlandish welcome wagon. Approaching the houses on the perfect curve of our street, she had made a progress to their front doors and had, according to my mother, delivered each occupant a copy of the daily paper, ones randomly flung onto their lawns. She then rang each and every neighbor's doorbell and introduced herself to whoever was at home. (Had our bell been rung, too? If she had answered, my mother would have been cordial, and livid. More likely, she would have stayed silent behind the door, a hand trembling slightly, held to the right side of her chin, waiting for the ringing to cease.)

That was my mother's simple and hateful charge. I had been carefully told already that this was the way with Jews, insinuating themselves into where they didn't belong, getting things that they did not deserve. They were repulsive physically, as was Mrs. Immer, whose features my mother described with distaste and relish. When I eventually saw this woman, she seemed to look as undistinguished as any other housewife and mother, but to my own she was a harbinger of what exactly?

Throughout her muddy discourse, my mother continued to tremble with rage, a red flush lighting her up, her head animated by a slight shake all its own, one I had never not noticed. Later, she would describe this disturbance in her daily field to my father when he came home from work. He would look patient and reasonable, all the while seeming silently to assent to her views—after all, his Wall Street firm had one person who was Jewish and had narrowly missed being caught up by the SEC in a shady stock deal. This incident was often offered in evidence by my mother as proof of Jews' unscrupulous monetary drives and general financial untrustworthiness (the tone of her accounts often bore with them some inchoate sense of sexual trespass). My father may have also looked on with some distress, however, at her own disturbed self.

For most of that morning, my mother undoubtedly had stood her watch, perhaps first at the front door, possibly peering through an ever-so-slight crack. The rest of the first-floor view would have been blocked by azaleas, rhododendrons, and mountain laurels; it was spring and they would have been in flower. The obstruction of the shrubs would have caused her to go upstairs and pass from room to room, as if patrolling a parapet, in order to survey Mrs. Immer's pursuit of her neighborly rounds. If Mrs. Immer did such a circuit at all, that is. Even then I suspected that early in the morning her vision may have already begun to become clouded by gin, a small lipstick-tinged measure of which she kept above the kitchen sink. I also knew that, prior to those daintily sipped offices, there was some more finely distilled essence of doubt and loathing regularly coursing through her.

Nevertheless, I have no trouble recollecting at any time the total, never unalloyed, love I felt for my mother. My earliest memories, in fact, are ones of viewing her through the open door of her room down the end of a long hallway, where she would sit naked at her vanity table, her attitude revealing a back not even Ingres had painted the likes of. Her door and mine then were never closed, the distance foreshortened in my psyche. Later, as I got older, access to her room had shrunk to a small, still tantalizing opening, while my own became dead closed. But, earlier, I desired nothing so much as to stay by her side, for she was often so oddly incorporeal that I had to be in her presence to keep her from slipping away.

I had been her constant companion, joyously helping her with the household chores so that we might remain together in the morning. We would housekeep, she vacuuming, I following with a carpet sweeper, marveling at the light and dark swathes created by the two spiraling roller brushes. In the basement, we would fold laundry and roll socks, and, when they needed darning, we would sit, side by side in the kitchen, our thimbles steadily pushing needles through my father's black cotton and argyle knit socks. When we weren't busy, I knew how to wait out her periods of silent distraction, expecting eventually to attend to her complaints of the day, as I had that one afternoon a few years later. As her regular, and often only, listener throughout the day, I had known about Jews, long having been schooled in their subtle ways, while inwardly starting at some of her epithets.

Normally, I was the model student for her lectures on life. When my mother told me of the days when she was a long-legged, athletic, and pretty girl, I was attentive and avid for more tales of idyllic summers in the Taconic Mountains of New York State, where she and her sisters would swim naked in the small lake by their house. She taught me all that I knew about nature— demonstrating how to string bright red dogwood berries into necklaces, how one could suck the nectar from the honeysuckle's flower, and how my preference for butter was revealed by her holding of a buttercup under my chin; I would feel the hot illumination of their reflected petals. Our backyard was something of a preserve, as I think my father kept it that way, for her, as a partial reminder of her summers and in contrast to the totalitarian manicures other yards were subject to. It was populated by wild, light-hungry pines, tall white oaks, and giant tulip trees that rose and rose, making all others small.

Our going into that untouched arbor was the beginning of a field trip into the world of small, overlooked, and marvelous things. In the dark of the pines, she would show me the aptly named Jack-in-the-Pulpit plants, whose single, wide leaf, tapered like a stretched, backward curving tongue, formed a canopy over its erect, white crayon of a pistil, harboring bunches of bright red berries at its base. Sometimes there was the even more rare Indian Claypipe, a thin, waxy apparition, ending in its curved vulviform bowl, the whole thing looking as if it had just been stuck, stem first, into the leaves and the loamy earth underneath by one of the town's seventeenth-century settlers hurriedly on his way through the forest in pursuit of an errand. An animist's love of this world of leaves and flowers has stayed with me, and I have tried to reveal some of its deeper essence to my sometimes bemused, but empathetic, sons.

However, in that other obsessive and unbalanced course of instruction, I was repelled by her classifications and never, I think, absorbed a single particular. I remained silent in the face of this teaching, and my mother may even have been aware of something like disapproval. There was falseness of tone somewhere in such possessed monologues. Unlike the natural world that had so infused and inspirited her early childhood, there were never specifics to this otherness that she was indicting. The word itself, "Jew," was meant as its own argument and conclusion. It seemed, too, though, that something shriveled and crumpled had formed the tinder for this peculiar burning.

Her rage seemed to have come from some imposed, vast inner

emptiness, its source, perhaps, an unhealed place of grievance about the injustice of who got what. It may have been a wound so regularly reopened to be made beyond healing. Somewhere in my childhood, I started to puzzle out, never successfully, what drove this woman of strong Quaker background from Philadelphia, and who was educated in Quaker schools, to such depleting frenzies.

She had more than a little pride in her in being one of the Society of Friends. Early on, I knew about the quiet services and the inner light, the plain architecture of the meeting houses, along with the quaint forms of address, the endearing "thee's" and "thou's." All elements of a small, close community, sustained, and not self-righteous, in its solitude. For a suburban wife and mother, however, this sufficiency of simple things was no longer enough, thus her juxtaposed and invidious references to superstitious Catholics, their smudged penitent foreheads, the suffocating incense, the hermetic Latin services, and the fact of their breeding, manufacturing four, five or more children.

Outside this crazy quilt of prejudice, however, she was utterly catholic in her reverence for human courage in the face of injustice and oppression. When I was able to read fairly well, she gave me her copy of the 1928 Literary Guild edition of *Black Majesty*, the story of Henry Christophe's role in the overthrow of the French occupation of Haiti and of his flawed efforts to create a peaceable kingdom there. (Returning home one college vacation, I noticed that she had long had in her possession a first edition of Richard Wright's *Black Boy* on her bookshelf.) I seem to have always known from her of Sibelius's very public opposition to the Nazi occupation of Norway, his hatred of Quisling, and how the composer's tone poem, *Finlandia*, became an anthem of national resistance in the same manner that

Verdi's "Va, pensiero," with its chorus of enslaved Babylonian Jews calling out for deliverance, acted upon Italians almost one hundred years earlier. Equally imprinted on me by her was the story of Denmark's king wearing the yellow Star of David, and how other Danes followed suit, in order to keep Jews from being identified and sent to death camps. And so, too, a love of courage is my inheritance from her; seeing it, my calm invariably deserts me.

Devotees of Rodgers and Hammerstein (and whose ethnicity passed without mention), my mother and father saw as many of the premieres of their musicals on Broadway as possible, and we possessed a number of the original cast albums. *South Pacific* was my mother's favorite, loving as she did the baritone of Ezio Pinza. She often pointed out to me the meaning of the young Lieutenant Cable's short song, "Carefully Taught," a burning, reckless waltz where he recounts to Emile DeBeque the corrosive instruction in bigotry one needs when young in order to become a thorough-going racist.

> You've got to be taught to hate and fear.
> You've got to be taught from year to year,
> It's got to be drummed into your dear little ear—
> You've got to be carefully taught . . .
> You've got to be taught before it's too late,
> Before you are six or seven or eight,
> To hate all the people your relatives hate—

It was almost as if these examples of courage and tolerance allowed my mother to step away from herself, to show a purer side, although she seemed unaware of any contradictions in what she was doing.

Perhaps part of this lack of self-awareness might be laid to the fact that she felt that the past was the creation of fabulists, and was, perhaps like her summers, a region somewhere else and separate. People *then* were part of a human family, albeit one white and Protestant. The present was different, oppressively immediate. Negroes, Catholics, and Jews were no longer beyond the pale. And, unlike the first two groups, Jews seemed to move up so quickly. They possessed money, gained education, flooded the professions, and claimed upper-middle class status, along with its most visible emblem, stately, relatively old, houses. Such as the ones our town of Manhasset displayed. Such as our house, whose kitchen I entered that late afternoon after school.

Manhasset was just another part of East Egg, and, although it was considerably to the south of the area toward which Gatsby wistfully gazes, most of the town's residents seemed to have had it made and were still on the rise; in fact two different neighbors of ours became heads of the nation's largest brokerage houses and moved their families more to the north, closer to the aura of the green light. Manhasset itself had always been old and moneyed, boasting such families as the Paysons, the Paleys, and the Whitneys, and their Negroes lived, and their children went to the first six grades of school, in a part of the town known as "The Valley," an area not far from their employers' estates. The town was further divided into a number of exclusive villages, such as ours, Munsey Park, the name being a corrupt version of the Algonquin language, Munsee, spoken by Delaware tribes long ago.

In the 1950s, Manhasset had begun to receive an influx of Jews (and who were, what I now realize, a very small number), who located themselves largely in the newer residential areas. Only a few found themselves in older neighborhoods such as ours, which had formerly been farmland and pasture, where several of the houses still had property lines marked out by a few stranded cedar posts, with rusting squares of fence wire. The Immers must have been very isolated, indeed. Nevertheless, those of us in the third and fourth grades at the Munsey Park School thought of all this somehow as an invasion, and we eight- and nine-year-olds were often no better than our parents, chanting "Guns to the Arabs, sneakers to the Jews" to what were at most four or five timid little girls. A combination of teachers scolding, boredom, and the fact that none of us knew what we were referring to, soon had us losing interest in this incantation. Like a lot of us, I'm not always at my best in crowds. Luckily, I was wiser at home.

Somehow within this very slight social flux, my mother must have sensed the tremors of a larger upheaval, and my father must have silently signaled agreement. What we needed was something impregnable and on higher ground. The result was the purchase of a summerhouse in a New Jersey lake community governed by a long series of restrictive covenants, a contradiction no one seemed to notice or care about. The town's name was Sparta, and only the elected few were permitted within its gates. The list of who was excluded could have been compiled from the seething pages of Father Coughlin's *Social Justice*. The usual suspects, of course, were out— Jews, Hispanics, and Blacks (my small defiance as a teenager was to drive by boat Henry, my fellow caddy, from the golf club where we worked to the lake's public boardwalk, much to the chagrin of local police). But the palisades were also raised against Eastern Europeans, Indians—both those native to this place and also those from the Indian subcontinent—, and Italians. The Irish were allowed some liminal position on the borders.

With all this vigilance and control, it didn't surprise me that our lake, Lake Mohawk, was manmade, bulldozed into existence in the 1930s and fed by underground springs, and then later choked by underwater weeds as phosphorous and nitrogen from lawn fertilizer leached steadily into it.

These undemocratic vistas, to my mother, though, were a point of pride and the excluding index—and the 1950s were notorious for these kinds of things—was usually her preamble for visitors to a full declaration of the virtues of having a summer home. The list also forever soiled my parents' ostensible purpose in buying a house on a lake, which was to recreate and re-evoke my mother's lost girlhood summers and pass some of their wonder on to my sister and myself. My mother, in fact, seemed to admit that there was something contrived in all this Christian enclosure, as she frequently referred to the lake as being "artificial," and perhaps it corresponded to the greater artifice of trying to reclaim that which could never be recovered.

And while Jews could be avoided and ignored, the subject of Jews never went away after that spring afternoon in the family hallway. By the seventh grade, the beginning of what was then called junior high school, I was getting regular and no-so-subtle counsel about "choosing" my new friends with greater care, about recognizing who was "sound," a Republican leitmotif of approval, and who was not. These vague warnings became harsher injunctions with my use of the Yiddish phrase, "*oy vey*," an expletive I'd picked up in school, which happily popped out of me at the slightest opportunity. Beyond being mildly reminded of the distinctions between "shall" and "will" and "can" and "may," I had never been linguistically double-teamed before, but other parents must have come down hard on their children, too, as the phrase vanished within weeks. Perhaps even more appalling, the Jewish kids no longer used it either, their parents perhaps wanting to secure themselves within middle-class America and desiring no public reminders of their own parents' or grandparents' neighborhoods in the Bronx or the lower East Side of New York. I didn't start stocking up on a rich lexicon of Yiddish until I got to college and joined a largely Jewish fraternity.

I did, nevertheless, have a Jewish friend, who lived among Jewish neighbors in one of the town's other exclusive villages, this one named Strathmore—Scots for a wide river valley; another bit of developer's legerdemain for terrain that was in fact hilly. I refused to give him up, even if I was compliant about my diction. It was also about this time when the Holocaust was being cautiously rediscovered (although no mention was made of it through my five succeeding grades of junior and senior high school). Peter had some glimmerings of it, and these he often passed on to me. One day, while we were buying Cokes at the neighborhood pharmacy and seeing if we could steal anything, he went directly over to the store's small paperback section and pulled out a book he seemed familiar with, for there was no hesitation in his reach. He turned to its picture section, which fell open from many previous openings and closings, and handed it to me, saying, I think, nothing. Displayed before me were page after page of black and white photographs of starving, empty-eyed men in striped pajamas, row upon row of stone autopsy tables, an endless series of barred brick ovens, and heaps of ghostly, impossibly thin bodies, pale kindling dumped every which way in new-dug earth. His parents wouldn't allow him to buy such books, he finally said.

Peter was a sore point for my parents, and he rarely came home with me. Not only was he Jewish, his grades were even worse than mine, and it didn't require much observation to detect the semi-circular, yellow-brown nicotine stains between his second and third fingers. Our time together would be mainly spent at his house, both of us smoking, playing our instruments, listening to the drumming of Art Blakey, Sam Woodyard, Shelly Manne, and Buddy Rich. Occasionally, Pete would play a Lenny Bruce album; Bruce's routines baffled me, knowing as I did nothing about sex, drugs, or being Jewish. Peter would accompany Bruce's monologues with knowing snuffles; Bruce drove his parents crazy, this Jewish boy who was blatantly skewering bourgeois sensibilities and aspirations.

My life became filled with daily, minor skirmishes with my mother, with lots of sniping over Jews. She kept trying to add to my education. Liberals (I was becoming one of them) were Jews, I was told, and teachers (I would become one later) were liberals. Although not all teachers were Jews. All Communists were Jews, though, and the fate of the Rosenbergs came as no surprise, for, on the front page of *Newsday*, they looked a lot like the parents on the corner. But no matter how explosive her charges, there was never anything between us that came close to a serious discussion of differences. That would have been too threatening to the pact between us, that she could go halfway into nothingness, and I would make sure, which I couldn't, that she didn't complete the journey. She still very much needed me as her listener, recounting her childhood summers and giving me small confidences about my father's business. But beyond the confines of teller and listener, we didn't know what to do with one another; perhaps it was rather like being married.

Much later, I began to have Jewish girlfriends and then a Jewish wife, although not a one was fully so. Almost all the women I dated were equal parts Jewish and Protestant, as if I were trying to establish the more perfect union I couldn't find at home. I remember my father, who was at heart quite diffident, asking through his nervous laugh about my fiancée, saying, "Is Monica Jewish?" When I answered yes, he replied, "Your mother thought so." My mother still prided herself on her ability to detect Jewishness, claiming she could "always tell." The earlier parrying of my teens was as nothing to my mother's anti-Semitic slurs aimed not-so-indirectly at my wife one evening in a restaurant. She passed an offhandedly venomous insult, leaked out in a drunken moment of verbal incontinence, which resulted in Monica's heading to the bathroom in tears. I did what I didn't have the courage to do until then. Surprising myself, then more husband than son, I demanded an apology, warning her that one more insult and I would not return home again. I was direct with her for possibly the first time. She knew I was serious, and she became contrite. There was even a mumbled apology. And the sniping stopped.

But, here again, I think the anti-Semitism was a mask for feelings of displacement. Of course, much of the insult to my mother wasn't that I'd married somebody Jewish; the greater betrayal was that I had married, period. I had, it seemed, broken our pact by joining with a woman so apparently foreign to her. My choice was also, then, a criticism of a kind of bitterness I was supposed to imbibe, but luckily never did.

Of course, I was kidding myself about marriage providing a degree of separation from my mother. I had merely silenced her. Monica and I still wound up driving from New York out to Long Island almost every weekend, eating on less-than-clean china, sleeping on sheets impregnated with dust, as our domestic of more than two decades had become more drinking partner for my mother than someone employed to do housework. My father both knew and didn't want to know what was happening. He felt helpless and only succeeded slightly in getting my mother to cut back a bit, switching from gin to white wine, after she had been hospitalized for a week with chronic liver problems (not too much later, she began furtively making spritzers by adding white wine to Fresca, a grapefruit soda).

The anti-Semitism would every once in a while still body forth. And where do I think that anti-Semitism came from? I can't pretend that it didn't do great damage. Nevertheless, as ugly as it sounded, it wasn't, I believe, Jews *per se* who had created such deep turmoil in my mother. I think I slowly saw what drove her along this ugly course only after she had died, and I had divorced, been singly and agonizingly alone, and then had, much later, remarried and had two children of my own.

My mother lived, I think, in almost continual, and inarticulate, fear that she was about to be pushed aside, believing she was someone completely without qualities or consequence. I remember her complaints of uppity "Negroes" newly arrived from the South and of Puerto Ricans (pronounced "porta rikkins") elbowing her aside in the subways and department stores of New York. Probably no less or more obnoxious than any other hurried segment of an urban population, these intruders embodied her fear that she would be shut out beyond the margins of the world. In the city, she felt without agency. This *dis*ease was no surprise to me, as she would periodically inform me of yet another outrageous brush with broad immigrant shoulders. The news was, after all, coming from a woman who refused to ride certain afternoon westbound trains of the Long Island Railroad into Pennsylvania Station in New York City. The 4:18, 4:33, and 4:41, when they stopped at Great Neck, the station just after ours, apparently transported many of the domestics who had been working all day in other people's houses. My mother was afraid of being mistaken for a maid. No matter that she was wearing a fur, carrying an expensive handbag, and displaying a star sapphire on one finger and a diamond on another, she must have feared her disguise of social arrival would be seen through. Her whiteness, too, would be unmasked. As a result, she only took trains that left well after 5:00 p.m.

New York shouldn't have been an unfamiliar place for her, despite her Philadelphia origins. When she was twelve, her father died of tuberculosis, and her mother, with little means of support, was forced to divide up her five children. Two sisters and a brother were to remain with their mother in The City of Brotherly Love. The two other sisters, the youngest—Betty, my mother, and Mazie—were sent to live with a married aunt, Mrs. Chester R. Baird, who had a large apartment in the upscale Murray Hill district of New York City. The couple was relatively well off, and they had no children. Both seemed to care deeply about their two nieces, and it was "Auntie" to whom my mother regularly referred in recounting her childhood days.

Of her mother, not a word was said. If Betty had been cast out of the home, then she would be able to banish her own mother from memory. I had little sense that her mother, whose name I do not know, ever existed. Perhaps this was my mother's first experience of a restrictive covenant. The implied understanding that I grew up with was that neither I nor my sister should ever enquire into parts of my mother's childhood that she had not already told us about. The erasures and silences were not to be noticed. Sadly, one of those excisions included my sister, and the memory of her childhood presence has only randomly been available to me. In some subtle ways, my mother, in her world view of division and favor, conveyed the knowledge that I was very much her son and Jeanne was her father's daughter. Such a splitting resulted in another divisive covenant: evenings and weekends Jeanne was close to my father, and I had my mother most weekday mornings and afternoons. In fact, I lost my father almost entirely during these years.

What I know now, I learned years later from my father and much of that was pulled out of him from my second wife, whose curiosity about my mother seemed driven by what she had no hesitation calling my "appalling childhood." My father, though, knew how much his wife, whom he loved, had been damaged, for her own mother had almost no contact with the two daughters once they had left Philadelphia. My mother never attended her mother's funeral and never seemed to register the fact of her death, my dad telling me all this late in his life, when he was well into his eighties. Perhaps this refusal was revenge. More likely it was despair.

Her youthful summers, those always bright August seasons, she would repeatedly tell me about. Then, all the children would be reunited at the aunt's lakeside cabin, with mother and aunt sharing household duties. To the four sisters, the time was an idyllic blend of indolence and activity, sail boating, canoeing, and basking in the attentions of admiring boys. There was endless swimming, the sisters' grace in the water. My mother, especially, seemed born to inhabit the lake, plunging into it without disturbance of its surface. She could execute a jackknife—lightly touching fingers to toes in midair, then snapping straight open on the way down—entering the water like a coin. The small, slightly browning Kodak prints the sisters took of her show me a graceful girl inscribing a new alphabet upon the white sky.

At the beginning of September, the two sisters would accompany Auntie back to the row house on East 36th Street, but I doubt that my mother ever returned to Philadelphia, not even on holidays. The first severing must have been repeated unendingly as an unendurable fugue of joining and parting, the two girls broken off once again from the larger whole. This sundering became ever more painful; when she was eighteen, my mother's Uncle Reamy, husband of Auntie, died too. The father she never had—I was named for him. Later that year, as she had planned, my mother left for college in upstate Troy, New York, a city only a few miles away from the cabin and lake of their summers. It may have been one leaving too many. She quit after the first semester and returned to New York to teach girl's physical education at The School for Ethical Culture, remaining safely in Auntie's house, leaving only to go to work.

Several years later, in her early thirties, she met my father, who was living at home, too. In his constancy, she knew he would not leave her, and in his robust health he was guaranteed not to die. The summers of those years, when she was away as a camp counselor off the coast of Maine during June and July, her own devotion was impressive. I have the blue letters that she sent him, the text sometimes composed in giddy spirals; all were saved in chronological order by him (her return address gives her name as Betty Baird; she had dropped her mother's married name of Culbertson and only reclaimed it much later). She would write him daily (he would do the same), occasionally sending him telegrams if the matter, such as the possibility of his changing jobs, seemed urgent. She told him that whatever course he chose would be right. Throughout the summers of 1933, 1934, and 1935, the letters between them flowed, filled with declarations of her love (and often included wordplay on my father's financial career, "on account of account of I love you"). They were signed, almost engrossed, "Betty," the first letter composed of two right-ward, horizontal parabolas closed by a proximate slash farther to the right, a signature that won her the nickname of "3,1 (three-one)-etty."

The next year they married. My father must have offered her a kind of security she hadn't had the prospect of since she was a very little girl. He was on the rise, even though it was the Depression, and throughout the 1940s he continued to live a charmed economic life, unscathed by the war. His success brought him a large, distinguished house in an already well-established suburb on Long Island. With its thick, brownish-red, hand-hewn cypress shingles that glowed in the morning sun and registered every slight shift in the light, it was not unlike an elegantly large, and understated, Quaker meeting house. Of course, the same vector of success would project other families, including Jewish ones arriving after the Korean War, out from the city and its outer boroughs and into the suburbs of this country, creating a republic of lawns, if of nothing else.

My father had found his niche in the suburbs. He particularly loved raking the leaves from our long driveway down into the street, setting the great dry red, brown, and yellow heaps on fire, as the other men on the block were doing. They would all stand around, talking of business and "the market," politics, and sports, the piles flaming, sending gray-white smoke into the sky, obscuring the sun by noon. In the distance, you could just hear the deep pulse of the drums and the silvery trebles of the bells of the high school marching band practicing for the afternoon's football game.

But my mother? This arrival left her divided, I think. She certainly must have believed that she was safe at last from loss and displacement, although her rise in social class created an uncomfortable distance from her working-class siblings in Philadelphia. Luckily her sister, Mazie, lived only four miles away, where she, having married a ship's captain, spent most of her time alone with her young child. My mother and I, often after an urgent call for company, would regularly visit her small, dark-brick, two-bedroom house in nearby Douglaston. Unlike the often wild and impetuous baby sister of my mother's summer letters of the 30s, Mazie seemed as dark and brooding as the house's cramped interiors. The two sisters would eat fudge Mazie had made—from her summer letters I knew that both girls had always loved chocolate—and would sip gin while sitting on the couch and keeping an eye on Mazie's small toddler, who sometimes patrolled the plastic fencing of her playpen and sometimes docilely sat in its center nudging a toy (neither sister seemed particularly happy to have a girl for a child, and both unknowingly set out to abandon them). I would spend my time getting out of the house and into the light and wandering about the narrow, residential streets looking for different varieties of trees and for overgrown, vacant lots to explore. When the visits were over, I would sit in the passenger seat, silent as a husband.

At home, my mother always identified strongly with my father's success, but conveyed in many ways the sense that she wasn't entitled to it. She practiced odd and humiliating little economies, only buying on sale at the new E.J. Korvettes housedresses of the sort that housewives, or maids, wore when they were cleaning (the name, E.J. Korvettes, I would find out much later, was a contraction of "Eight Jewish Korean Veterans"). Evenings, she would tell my father with pride how she had saved. It was he—sensitive to, and trying to arrest, her growing impalpable self, I think—who would, on anniversaries, birthdays, and holidays, buy her jewelry to let her feel her worth and Persian lamb coats and mink stoles to help her feel covered.

I think, though, that nightmares never go away. They sit and wait to take their innings. Eventually, my mother was left all alone in a large house, slowly emptying of us as we left for college, and with my father hardly knowing how to help her. And she no longer was able to visit her beloved Mazie, who outstripped my mother in alcoholism and madness. Checking herself out of North Shore Hospital before recovering fully from acute appendicitis, Mazie was later discovered wandering senselessly in the nearby roadside woods. Not much later she died. My mother was then inconsolable, and her Philadelphia siblings were no replacement. My mother, Betty Baird Culbertson Jansen, began drinking more steadily than ever, possibly in pursuit of Mazie. In the home's vacuum, she created a life of dark fantasy, full of injuries and enemies. The brooding terror of displacement offered a constancy all its own. By the time distant Jewish neighbors arrived, chaos had become her night-blooming flower.

When I awoke one night to take the call from my father that she had died instantly from a massive heart attack, while drinking with a neighbor at the lake, I was relieved. Monica and I would no longer have to make those undutiful trips to Manhasset that I couldn't cut away from. I was finally rid of her. I could, at last, be free. I was disconcertingly elated, and we simply went back to sleep. She was buried in a small ceremony, although I do not know where, arranged by my father and her one remaining sister. In her will, she left my sister, Jeanne, all her jewelry, but there were no material things that she could pass on to me, except for a few books, such as *Black Majesty*, that I had cared for and possess to this day.

ARSENIC

In a place where I spent much of my childhood was a place my mother called the vegetable room, so named for the large rectangular pine box suspended from the ceiling and whose chicken wire bottom and wood dividers held separate amounts of onions, carrots, and potatoes, the protruding eyes of which, the beginnings of shoots, I would be responsible for, blinding them with a thrust of my childish thumb. Eventually, the bins fell into disuse, vegetables becoming packages going into the frozen north of a new refrigerator still called an icebox. Underneath the bin remained a stack of split firewood, dusty and brittle, never put to use in our living room fireplace.

The room's other side held a looming wooden, freestanding closet that didn't hold much of anything, reels of 16-mm home movies shot by my father and some black and white Woody Woodpecker cartoons. It was only later that, after my father had quietly moved the Fleischmann's gin from the kitchen pantry and onto the shelves of the closet, he screwed a flimsy-looking hasp onto the closet's door—the wood screws going in like bad teeth. The hasp accommodated a small lock. Periodically, I would take out the screws to see if anything interesting—something needing hiding, other than gin, which was of course not truly hidden—was spirited away onto the shelves.

Other parts of the room received a fair portion of my father's stuff, a somewhat scattered archive, mainly back issues of *The Wall Street Journal*, from which he had taken clippings, and *Barron's Financial Weekly*, for which he contributed quarterly articles on transportation securities, covering mostly railroads in a time of their on-going decline (some of his lamenting headlines included "How Good Are Rail Earnings?," "Tortuous Progress," and "More Dead Weight.")

The vegetable room, though, was my known habitat, where I'd later venture down to look over my father's books from his high school days, some titles being Scott's *Rob Roy*, small volumes of Macaulay's essays on Warren Hastings and Lord Clive, *Washington Merry-Go-Round*, and two volumes of Peter Arno cartoons from *The New Yorker*, several of which would have been considered "spicy." One time I even foolishly tried to write French using his water-stained French-English dictionary. Something plaintive perhaps: *Je suis ici*

Over a bit of time, though, I'd added some of my own things, such as a basic store-bought mineral collection, its small samples glued to labeled compartments of the kind that would have held assorted chocolates from Schraft's: malachite, obsidian, black, thin peels of mica, a chunk of lead that wrote like a carpenter's pencil, pyrite ("fool's gold"), and a stringy gray lump of asbestos, which I knew was deadly and which I teased away strand by strand, nevertheless.

The vegetable room became my legitimate science room once I received a Gilbert chemistry set, although I felt the absence of the helpful lab assistant-father assisting the boy pictured on the cover of the instruction manual. Chemicals in combinations succeeded mainly in mishaps. Later, my friends and I tested various sorts of solid rocket fuel purchased from an unsuspecting Edmond Scientific, with one home-made batch endlessly smoking like a Pennsylvania tire fire and sending a grainy, breath-denying miasma up into the kitchen, flavoring my mother's cooking for the day.

Still, the most dangerous of materials had been residing in the house well before we took our occupancy—a large container in the shape of a good-sized mayonnaise jar. It was, of course, out of the way in plain sight on an upper shelf to the right of the vegetable bin and which I'd eventually noticed in my continual progress through the house's interiors.

Not quite a jar in Tennessee, it nevertheless possessed a squat gnomic presence. In my chemistry phase I was able to take it down and read its label more closely—A r s e n i c—and I still remember that 454 grams equal one pound. That's all I can recollect of the text side of things, although I'd like to say that there was a black skull and cross bones somewhere on its surface. Such piratical emblems were common in 1950s households—iodine for cuts and scrapes, although curiously all right when a component of table salt; household cleaning products, such as carbon tetrachloride.

Upon twisting open the lid—and I worried about what might body forth from this vessel—what I saw was a violet-tinged, fine gray powder about which I never gave the slightest thought of possibly inhaling, although I did afterward furiously wash my hands in the adjoining laundry room with powdered laundry detergent, Oxydol. Of a lethal color, or perhaps more a tint or a taint that had not yet solidified over the years before I opened it, it drifted out like any fine substance once the jar was disturbed. And, yes, while I continually prodded it with a pencil, I also assayed the powder between thumb and forefinger, an act succeeded by further anxious ablutions.

That was pretty much it regarding physical contact with the jar and its contents, which I returned to its upper shelf. Safely out of the way, though, the object had established an equally secure place in my mind where it did hold dominion off and on through the rest of my adolescence. Because it was poison, of course. I could, I knew, poison my parents. I knew this in a general way—parents, poison; poison, parents. From seeing Basil Rathbone as Sherlock Holmes, I knew that arsenic presented the taste of bitter almonds and so one couldn't just sprinkle the powder over morning cereal without remarks about the cyanotic color let alone the bitter, nutty taste, and my parents didn't eat cereal anyway. Still, that's what its purpose was, to poison parents. Not a parent, a mother or a father, or my father or my mother, although this would have solved the always resistant, insoluble difficulty of gin.

I'd also seen *Arsenic and Old Lace* on our black and white television in yet another part of the basement, and so I knew that the powder was a polite, somewhat eccentric, slightly dotty, really close to harmless when one thought about it, offered without malice, but nevertheless an always quick and fatal kind of poison. Unsuspecting dinner guests simply and gracefully keeled over in a few hours time in their rooms fully dressed (later in my reading as an undergraduate, Emma Bovary's horrifying, tormenting, days'-long death— "God! It's horrible!" says Emma, who, "soon began to vomit blood"—put the lie to arsenic's benign reputation).

The room itself at some point slipped out of existence, although the jar remained secure in its niche. It was there in the way that my fielder's mitt was in the back of my closet, perhaps in keeping for the right season. It was there, too, in my final years of high school when I'd sometimes lean forward pressing my waist against the guard rail over the single track of the Port

Washington line of the Long Island Railroad, whose afternoon trains returned with commuters like my father or headed west to take mothers into the city and on to Broadway for the theater.

VOICES: HOW I BECAME A SENSITIVE SOUL

I listened to Peter and The Wolf on my 78.
Each time I played the last side I hoped the duck would finally get out.

I believed my mother when she told me I could see the faeries dancing in the snow down below my bedroom window.

My first school was dark and expensive. I was dazed for two years.

I kept hoping we would pick pumpkins in the garden kids talked about but couldn't see.

I would dance in my soft brown Capezzios when Miss Staples played "Country Gardens" on the piano in our first grade classroom. The public school I could walk to.

The conductor was Serge Koussevitzky.

I believed my mother would write a book. She said she would. I should write a book, she said. About cheeses, she said.

I wanted to pat my baby sister on the head. My aunts said no it would hurt her.
Be gentle they said.

My first doctor was a woman.

My mother said you haven't lived if you haven't sailed.

My father taught me how to pour wine at dinner.

I collected leaves for a book, maple, oak, dogwood, sassafras, cherry.

The voice was Richard Hale.

I saved early for my mother for Christmas. Teaspoons one year.
Chinese vases the next.

I watched the blue window as sunset carved the light from my room.

I should write a book. About wine, my mother said.

I watched my father use big scissors to cut out green pieces of paper.
Are you making money? I said.

One morning my mother raised a red flag and waved.

My father and I drove to the Bronx Zoo. I sat in the front both ways.

I inventoried the trees in our yard. Three oaks, three elms, six pines, a dogwood, and two dying hollies. Both the same sex.

I mustn't wake my mother up in the afternoon. She sleeps naked on the chaise longue.

I should write a book about cheeses. You haven't lived until you've had Camembert.

My odalisque.

I planted a garden by myself on the east side of the house. I cultivated the soil.

From seed packets I planted dusty millers, marigolds, blue morning glories, yellow asters, black-eyed susans.

We write our names in tar in the street with sticks.

I hit my best friend with a metal rod. My mother said I would go to a reformatory.

My father told me the secret to a good martini.

I memorized the string quartet that was Peter. In C.

I sang O Holy Night at the school recital. My candle was a small bulb attached to a D battery I could just hold.

I got a Kodak Brownie and took pictures of my sister and our dog.

I punched my friend Bobby in the head.

You pass the cap of the Vermouth bottle over the shaker.

Sides 3 and 4, Victor Red Seal Records, of Peter and the Wolf broke. The broken record is what I have.

I was called The Terrible Tempered Mister Bangs.

Also Ferdinand the Bull who sat in the shade of a cork tree and smelled the clover. I forgot that.

I threw the hardest pitches of anyone but was afraid of teams.

I planted mint for my parents' clear drinks.

We had a currant bush in our garden. You haven't lived until you've made jam, my mother said.

I still have the album. Peter faces front, his round face smiling. He's wearing a red jacket, a black cap and boots. His arms are out like he's going to float.

My neighbor saw my garden and gave me a pot of Scottish bluebells.

I planted them in the shade of an oak and tended them for years.

Outside, a kid said, don't you know who that is that's reamy jansen.

A photo of my mother and me I tore in two. Her side she found in my wastebasket.

I had to tape them together. I'm listening to Steve Reich, It's Gonna to Rain. The voice is Brother Walter's.

I should write a book on wine, my mother said.

II

My personal opinion is that the photographer should be more concerned with the quantity and quality of *reflected light* that is returned from the subject to the observer or to the camera . . . than with the incident light that illuminates the subject.

Various subjects reflect varying amounts of light. The brighter an object appears, the more light it is reflecting to the observer. The more light an object absorbs, the less it reflects, and the darker it appears.

—Ansel Adams, *The Negative*

AVAILABLE LIGHT: NOTES ON GOING BLIND

Blinded by the Light

Being blind sometimes means being enveloped not by darkness but, rather, being possessed of too much light. One can become dazzled, with light unmaking the world, leaving it overexposed, browning, and beyond recall. Leaving one staring at the sun. Such was my first encounter with not being able to see, of being blinded by light.

My eye doctor, having discovered my middle-age glaucoma and checked its slow, destructive pressures, decided to send me forth to a retina specialist, retinas tending to detach in my family, offering only half worlds until put back in their place. (Such an event once occurred to my father while playing tennis, and he was left, literally, with a half-court game.) The examination itself brought no surprises—these curved walls would not come tumbling down. Not yet, this doctor said, perhaps not ever. But in order to have his look about, it had been necessary to dilate my pupils out to what felt like the diameter of a penny, and on leaving his office I had to shield my eyes even to negotiate its soft gray carpeting.

Outside is a hot July New York noon, and the light hits me with the force of several suns. Brilliance is everywhere and unavoidable. I shrink from it, head retracting protectively, hand futilely shading my eyes. The sidewalk becomes a desert with no horizon, and my ten-block trek north to the cross-town bus has me looking to others as if I'm battling a gale known only to myself. The trip back is one of tactile uncertainty and continual flinching. After an hour, I arrive home. Safe. Several hours later, my eyes have returned to normal. Nevertheless, I have been burned.

The Blue Light

At the age of sixteen I failed the eye test for my driver's permit by misreading the solid block letters of the chart's third line from the top: A B P F becoming A E F P. I should not have been surprised by this miserable performance, for I had known, though not believed, that my vision even then had deteriorated markedly, a situation, though, that I'd mentioned to no one. I could no longer read the blackboards in my tenth-grade classes and was stumbling badly in subjects that didn't require a printed text. Fearfully alert to any slight signs of my mortality, I had nevertheless developed a compensatory ability to fend off such troubling physical realities.

So finely tuned was this capacity for self-deception that I came to believe the chalk used in the classroom was of a particularly inferior sort. Geometry was no longer a matter of sharply drawn triangles and trapezoids, their angles filled in with degree markings, but one of figures that were, rather, a maze of thick, foggy, and indeterminate lines. I never seemed to catch on to the fact that the blackboard came into focus each time I passed it on the way out of class; the short distance between two points held no insight.

Interned in adolescent hell that year, perhaps I had already given up hope. So eye doctors became a bit like secular saviors, and I still remember the thrill at being able again, with glasses, to read a simple street sign. I was once more oriented to a world with clarity and perspective. Nevertheless, many of my inchoate fears about how ungrounded I felt began to focus on the vulnerabilities of my eyes.

A few years later, needing a new eyeglass prescription change just after I had crossed the meridian from teen to nominal adult, I paid a visit to my father's ophthalmologist. This was the first visit I had ever made alone to a doctor, and it brought me in contact with a heliophobe who kept his office as dark as a movie theater.

Once my eyes had adjusted, though, his office revealed just the right amount of reassuring male squalor of cracked, button-burst leather furniture, and poorly stacked, perpetually cascading journals and files. It looked, in fact, pretty much like my dad's office on Wall Street. And the examination itself proceeded as a predictable mix of magic lantern show, with boldface letters being projected rather than shadow puppets, accompanied by a cadenced elliptical patter involved in the twirling and selecting of lenses ("this, or *this?*"), a process sustained until the crispest image was determined.

The unnerving part of the examination came last, with my first test for glaucoma. This procedure involved a simple machine that, to the testee, comprised a metal chin rest and headband and slightly resembled the iron restraints once used to harness the insane. At its other end were the controls, with a knob that moved toward me a metering device that would rest against my eye and record its pressure. To accomplish this docking of mechanism and eyeball, I would open wide my slightly anesthetized eye while fixing its gaze on a blue "target light"—an illumined, protruding circle that burned as brightly as a newly struck kitchen match. Having no knowledge then of this device and its operation, I came close to fainting, fearing that the instrument enclosed a needle readied to pierce my cornea in accomplishing its purpose. After all, the three concentric circles inscribed within the blue sphere resembled an archer's target. Some minutes later, after a series of slow breaths and being restored to close to normal consciousness, the test was complete. Glaucoma proved then not to be a worry.

By the time I was forty, I had become an experienced and casual hand with the blue light.

Legacies

In looks, I am my mother's son—a Culbertson through and through. Tallish and big boned, we tend to loom over others and fill up a room. We all have noses as distinctive as Bob Hope's or Richard Nixon's, and thin, tight, disapproving mouths that reveal our Scottish Presbyterian roots, ones that arc downward into a readiness to project a fated, gloomy view of the world. Also, the lot of them seem to possess 20/20 vision. Eyeglasses are unknown.

My father's chromosomal contributions are less visible. Foremost is the legendary "Jansen memory," which I see manifest in my information-absorbing sons. The other legacy, glaucoma, I hope will pass them by. When its presence is revealed to me, my father apologizes, for he feels personally responsible for this bad roll of the loaded genetic dice. Montaigne in his forties was also surprised at the painful inheritance of his father's kidney stones, whose presence was previously "concealed," and he was bemused as to how it was that only he, among all his siblings, should find himself the recipient of "this slight bit of substance, with which he made me, (and which should) bear so great an impression."

Glaucoma becomes a new, late onset bond between father and son. We now compare eye tests, and, invariably, I am the one to take him for eye checks, and once for laser surgery—looking on as light lances the cornea of his eyes, leaving their surfaces forever delicately slit, if one wants to look closely. The operation is the last attempt to retard the on-going destruction of his optic nerve. Its effects, though, have merely been *son et lumiere.*

My first awareness of this potential and degenerative estate comes in 1955, when my mother descended to our house's cavernous basement, a place where, since early childhood, I had staked my claim to what were various dim and barren play areas. That year I was a habitue of what I liked to think even in those pre-Sputnik days was my subterranean science laboratory. But as much as these lower rooms furnished me with enlightenment about crystals, cells, and explosive chemicals, this domain functioned more as an area where I could withdraw, although it may also have resembled the place of a child hiding noticeably, hoping for discovery. My mother's appearance in my underworld was an occasion, for I had felt invisible in this house more often than not, a small moon, unregistered and detached from the parental orbit. "Your father is going blind," were her only words before trembling and tears, and I knew that my job, at age twelve, was to console, which I did ineptly, I think. She wanted me to hold her. But we had never touched, not that I can remember.

What frightened her were imagined scenes of my father blinded, no longer striding with determination and commercial vigor to the Long Island Railroad, but instead, becoming helpless. I knew, too, that she had images of financial ruin, for stock tickers don't print in Braille. In the back of my mind, I think what she feared most was that he would be home, forever seated in his armchair, a blind, broken and idle king. This prospect was an anxious image for me, too, for would I become even more the phantom to him than I thought I already was?

Of course, none of this dark drama came to pass immediately. There was, first, my mother's tendency to stampede a few facts in the most disastrous direction possible. Second, in reality, my father's condition could be treated simply with eye drops. But from that day forward I became a secret observer and sharer of my father's eye problems—retinas that would need reattaching, cataracts that had to be shaved away, drops that steadily increased in dosage, and, eventually, separate medicines that had to be applied to each eye. After one operation much later, the doctors seemed to have torn away part of his left iris to enlarge the light-resisting aperture. His eye became a ragged hole, petals ripped off in a child's clumsy grasp, and for some time I could not look him directly in the eye and was ashamed.

Such steady medical efforts maintained his vision into his late seventies, when, suddenly, other physical difficulties set his seeing on a rapid, unstable course. A black hole came to exist about thirty feet into his horizon—cars that he saw approaching this periphery would vanish as if part of the news footage of an earthquake. He more and more relied on a variety of lighted magnifying glasses, but eventually even the strongest lenses would fail him, and his eyes' interiors became his sole world. His cosmos was his own, with storm fronts breaking within those orbs, ones clouding independent of the weather. When he would ask me now and again if it was hazy out, I'd often lie and say yes (and how much now do I regret these not-so-small deceptions). The only way for his doctor to test his field of vision was to fasten fat clumps of white tissue paper to the wall of his office with map pins. Most of this improvised geography escaped him, and he was, finally, legally blind.

All's Right with the World

By the time I was in my mid-thirties, I had become anxiously single and was engaging in random glaucoma checks. At night and alone, driving or walking, I'd squint at the streetlights, looking for the telltale haloes presaging something amiss. I subjected myself to this activity when I was feeling particularly lonely and mortal. What I would see provided just the unsettling degree of ambiguity that I no doubt desired. And my nascent fear of blindness was not one whit diminished by the fact that year after year my eye pressure checks turned out to be fine.

As I entered my early forties, I had recast myself into a relatively responsible, and somewhat less fearful, married man. I had become a father, no less, of a three-and-a-half-year-old boy, whom I loved in a way I never could have foreseen. An invisible artery—what the Japanese call "a red thread"—was always there between us, and I watched over him all the time. But while I could transport this child of mine upon my shoulders for hours, I was also beginning to feel the gravitational tug of middle age.

More inhibiting to my bookish ways, though, was that I could no longer easily read with my eyeglasses on and, instead, had to pull the page to within a few inches of my eyes. Reading glasses awaited me, said friends who'd been that way before. I should avoid bifocals, I was told, for they made one look the dodderer before ever reaching fifty. Bifocals, though, were what I found I would require; I was just getting too nearsighted. That bit of news was the first, and manageable, consequence of visiting my eye doctor. But the eye-pressure test that was usually so *pro forma*—my annual gaze into the familiar blue light—now claimed center stage. My pressure was indeed finally up, and I was to be sent in a few days to the New York Eye and Ear Hospital for specialized tests—"tonography" and "field of vision." Both sounded benignly geographic, but I was not lulled into believing that I was going to brush up on earth science. This traversing of my globes, I knew, would be dire.

Tense with fear during this three-day interim, I drift in a haze. (I am particularly aware that my father's sight is failing faster at this point, for the thin, oddly-angled wire of his optic nerves have begun to fray and are finally snapping like fatigued bridge cables.) I clear myself of self-absorption one night later, though, while I am putting Paul to bed. I notice that his stuffed animals are neatly covered to their chins by crib blankets and are lined up at right angles to his mattress. Each doll has stickers over both eyes. "Their brains are sick," he tells me, and here I see how much I have been silently signaling my terror. The polar bears, pandas, and Curious George recover, albeit slowly at the rate of one animal a day, after I have assured this sensitive, sentinel of a boy that I'd be taking some eye tests that I needed for new glasses. He seemed calmed, and I was somewhat. Certainly I had not been blind to him.

Still, like my mother—long dead, but whose ideas of storytelling included Gothic tales of surgery at the turn of the century—I couldn't help but think about how grim these tests were likely to be. I imagined that tonography involved no less than the removal of my eyeball, with which medical technicians would play some sort of evaluative handball.

The following morning I headed off for the hospital, alone. The tests, when I actually submitted to them, proved less horrific than anticipated, as is occasionally the case with reality. Tonography involved a subtler reading of pressures than that offered by the regular office procedure, and the field of vision test was rather like a video game carried on inside a small planetarium.

Despite its arcade feel, though, this second test, I knew, was serious stuff—as it gauged how far one was away from that stage where the cars on the event horizon would eventually begin to disappear into nothingness.

Like many other eye tests, field of vision began with the ever-present chin rest, positioning the face just inside half of a sphere reminiscent of an oversized colander with holes the size of pinpoints. When the lights in the room went out, the lights within the half shell started to blink on and off, seemingly at random. For each light I saw, I was to depress the button on a hand-held buzzer of the kind used by players on the game show *Jeopardy*. It was difficult not to slip into a trance with this kind of thing or even lose consciousness entirely (and since childhood I had become an unaware master of this dissociative state). The half globe had a way of swallowing the world along with normal notions of space and time. Eventually I suspected that I was imagining lights where there were none, and I was equally unsure that the light I thought I was seeing was nothing but a visual echo of what I'd just seen. Were these imaginary stars in a real firmament? Rarely had I felt so engulfed, and just before I felt about to go under, the test was over. I scored well, the technician informed me. No black holes yet. No disappearing cars for now.

The Small Rain

But I did, according to the tonography results, have glaucoma. And while the pressures were only slightly over the borderline, I was conscious that this affliction had visited me ten years before it first came upon my father. The journey back to my apartment was a long one, filled as I was with awareness of a pumping pressure in my eyes, most likely, though, a mixture of eyestrain and self pity. Prescription folded away in my pocket, this day was to be the first that I would be taking eye drops twice daily for the rest of my life. The little 4 ml plastic dispensing bottle with its light blue cap had, in fact, been familiar to me since my teens; my father had always kept his in the egg tray in the refrigerator. My Sears Coldspot now would hold my very own bottle, cupped within an egg compartment. Morning and evening, I would have to extract the bottle, twist off its top, and pull my lower lid down, while with two fingers my other hand would squeeze the bottle poised above my brow to release one tiny bomb of a drop into the lower part of the eye. For a while, this activity ruled my day. It was as if I were injecting myself with insulin rather than splashing down a few curative drops. And also for a while I wanted no one to see me in what I took to be a humiliating rite, furtively performed. In the first days of my new offices I was continually reminded of my father putting in his drops and how exposed were his eyes as he did this, their surfaces glistening and trembling like fresh egg whites. He didn't seem to mind, but the watcher in me couldn't stand the nakedness of it all; I didn't want my boy to see me in this light.

When I Consider How My Light Is Spent

A short while ago, I sat for a computerized field of vision test and then watched while the laser printer marked the perimeters of a general visual field. The printout looked a bit like a stylized skull, its dull ghost-eyed blankness exaggerated by the absence of nose and mouth—only the eyes mattered on this visage. The lines that inscribed it were composed of finely printed numbers ranging from the twenties (good) down to their negative opposites (bad). The test offered up what might be bad news—I'm doing below-average work, something like a D, around my nasal periphery, that area where sight first flickers out. According to my doctor, who sounds reassuring, but hasn't quite got me convinced, it's probably no problem, and eye drops in greater dosages—ones at my father's current level (although he was in his eighties) should remedy the difficulty. And I guess I'm reassured enough.

I'm also conscious that at some, probably far off, point the world I now see may begin to abrade and ultimately may be scraped away the way a coin's edge strips the silver-gray coating off a lottery ticket. My consolation will be the knowledge—mine and my father's—that the phenomenal world might not be so substantial anyway. I've come close to seeing eye to eye with Ireland's first philosopher, Bishop Berkeley. I've decided that we not only see, but also construct, our worlds as best we can, inventing our lives in relation to whatever is out there. I know now that there are ways of not seeing that I will always have to be careful of and that there are darker blindnesses—"not only of woods and shady trees," as Frost's reflective farmer observes—that keep us from seeing trees falling in forests and from reading the faces of those who are beloved.

SLOWNESS

I seem to have inherited (or to have acquired more of since his death) my father's studied, and often maddening, deliberateness. The way he would have, say, of making sandwiches for the two of us during one of my infrequent afternoon visits. All was slow motion and time lapses, as he covered the small distance between counter and refrigerator, with each ingredient extracted separately from its particular location: the bread, the cheeses, meat of some kind, perhaps some lettuce going a bit limp. For the bread, he would remove four slices, rewrap the package his way, with the opening folded over on itself, and then return it carefully to its exact place on the shelf from which he had taken it.

He would resist my offers of assistance, perhaps sensing their similarity to the impulse—at first tender, then impatient, and, finally, infused by a slight shame—I often had in wanting to hustle him across New York City streets because the light had already turned to green. At home, he would walk and make things at his own pace. Next would be the unwrapping of cheese from foil, saved from a tiny quarto of the stuff stored in the closet and used again and again, giving the foil its finely worn, aged, and wrinkled surface. Cheese on bread, finally, he'd fold the foil once more, pressing lightly to keep it all in place.

The too-large cold cuts would be turned down neatly like the top sheet on his now-too-large double bed. Then back the remaining slices would go to the refrigerator, as I observed the faintly noticeable path he had worn through the once custardy yellow of the linoleum, now a slight, graying swale, no longer susceptible to polish.

And what it all amounted to was a modest, even meager, meal, with the elapsed time promising only the staleness of the bread. I snapped it up, at my far end of the dining table, in a few impatient, blind bites. He, however, would consume as he had created—slowly, reading the texture of the bread through his fingers, opening his mouth wide as a baby robin's for the sandwich half he could no longer see. Later, he would feel the crumbs on his plate, and he would then feel the paper of the plate. For him, it was a meal. There was a knowing, considered taste. But it was touch, the savor of things held between the fingers, that meant more.

It is only fitting, then, that as I write this out of doors on a green picnic table, I should want to return things slowly, one by one, dictionary, books, then pads, pencils, and, finally, this page. My pace is so unlike that of my helpful son, who, sensing some distress of mine, and assuming my acceptance of his offer of assistance, scoops up all the elements of my writing into a barely embraceable heap, and, while he heads for the back door, suddenly emits an apologetic "oops" as something falls to the earth and something else is blown away, never to be recovered.

HOUSEHOLD GODS

"things mortal touch the mind . . ."
Virgil, *Aeneid*

College summers, I often spent my spare time as literature's voluptuary, recumbent upon my parents' living room couch, dutifully attempting to fill the gaps in my survey courses with the reading of "great works." Even now, I can still feel the impress of rolled Regency arms just below my shoulder blades when, on languid Saturday afternoons, I would strain to stay interpretively awake as Porfiry Petrovich, one of fiction's first fatherly cops, skillfully grilled Raskolnikov, making his crime sound as if the guilty undergraduate had committed a pardonable category error in philosophy rather than the brutal axe murder of a pawnbroker.

It was *The Aeneid*, though, that most possessed me. I loved the seemingly simpler story, with its heroic meanderings of father and son, Aeneas and Achates, and their Mediterranean swashbuckling. I knew even then, however, that part of the book's appeal was the sustained tone of loss that underlay the most vivid of its scenes. *The Aeneid*'s dominant mood conveyed the sense that the past was unrecoverable, with attempts at its recollection inevitably leaving one filled with "tears for passing things," a remark that Aeneas makes to his son after the two have looked upon frescoes depicting a Troy that was no longer.

Despite my resonating with the epic overall, one passage puzzled me, particularly when I thought about the lines sometime later. They concerned Aeneas's rescue of his father, Anchises, as Troy was being sacked by vengeful Achaeans. On beating his retreat, my hero was not only carrying his father on his back, but, seemingly, he was also transporting the burden of the family's "household goods."

I think that it was here, in this image of Aeneas as a one-man moving van, that my idea of a son's duty was confirmed. Such filial heavy lifting, after all, was real heroism—carrying your dad and all his stuff, too.

I know, however, that, if I looked again at what I read close to thirty years ago, I would find that the correct phrase was household "gods" (*lares et penates*), not household "goods." I should point out, defensively, that such a confusion—goods as gods—is surely an American one. And even if I was wrong, then, I'm certain that Anchises never had a six-foot, living room couch that he insisted on taking with him on his move, severe fellow that he no doubt was.

Aeneas never had a Toyota station wagon, either. Which was what I, along with my two small sons, climbed into every Saturday morning and headed out to my father's large, suburban home of forty-five years, a place where I had spent childhood and beyond. For the suburbs, the house could be considered old. Built in 1929 by New York State's official architect for his own family, his professional touch was everywhere—in the house's thick and irregular hand-hewn cypress shingles, the bluish-hued slate roof, and where, inside, the hand-pegged oak floors had planks as wide as diving boards. In such an environment, I had learned beauty and proportion, of an aesthetic sort at least.

Finally, though, my father had sold the family home and wanted my sister and me to clear and clean it out so that he could move to her place in Connecticut. While I periodically diverted the boys with snacks, television, the temptations and imagined terrors of the attic and basement, my father and I would sift through, select, and occasionally throw out, enough paper to overflow a Brooklyn landfill. Everything that was retained got packed by me and labeled by him in wavering block letters, his marker riding over the slight waves of the corrugated sides of the cartons.

Most precious among the remaining bulk of brittle legal pads, stationery with an address no longer to be used, and faded examination blue books held over from his college teaching days, was a small, frail pocket notebook, dated 1980, a thing whose brief and varied notations caught in shorthand much of how he saw, and lived in, the world. Its pages provided comments on people he'd met—"Joe Trumbull. Gave me a lift to the station. Pleasant. Apparently in construction field." And even in old age he was still copying out examples of good prose, such as an excerpt from a nature essay he had read in *The Atlantic Monthly* and which was accompanied by an appreciative comment about the author's sure use of extended analogy. Creating broken cursive veins along the pad's rectangular pages were long lists of vocabulary still to be learned—"epiphany," "deja vu," "fortitude"— and which were sometimes set down with their contexts—"God is invisible and *ineffable.*" Seen through the leaves of this miniature commonplace book was the aspect of the striving boy from the Bronx, attending George Washington High School (his classmate was Lou Gehrig), improving himself out of the neighborhood by writing, going on to Columbia University, Wall Street, and then to the older, stately suburbs of Long Island, where he purchased the house we were now draining of things.

As more and more of the larger items were removed from the house's ground floor, however, I found myself walking in disoriented fashion through phantom couches, ectoplasmic tables and chairs, all the while hearing echoes of mortal footsteps previously muffled by expansive, oriental rugs and richly-textured drapes. As the furniture continued to vanish, my father continued to sit, an isolate in his remaining armchair in what had become a stately, barren, rectangular room. When I asked how he felt about all these absences, he told me he was reining in his emotions until later. Upon arrival in Connecticut, at my sister's, he said he'd be ready to unpack them, too.

A good deal of what seemed discarded, though, would return with me and the boys. We looked like New Age Joads as we journeyed West to New York City, the boys' cycles caught in the mandibles of the car's bike rack, bookcases strapped to the roof with their skyward shelves filled with area rugs and household oddments. The car's interior was always crowded with much that could not be parted with for no particular reason. I'm a sentimental hoarder. Perhaps all men are. My father's rather extraordinary collection of penknives went almost magically from his top drawer to mine. Men, one supposes, find it impossible to throw out items of this sort. For a while, to justify my accumulation, I carried three—one Army and two civilian others that were discreetly part of a bill clip and a key chain. I continued this practice until my pant pockets began to wear through from the gravitational pull of so much metal.

But, of course, there were lots of non-pocket-sized items that I was transporting, too—my grandfather's eight-drawer nail box, with his carefully hand-lettered labels ("Brads," "Bolts," "1 1/2 W. Nails" . . .), his ancient brace and bits, and wood-encased box planes. My father, who was also a hoarder, had easily seen into my heart's unresisting core as he loaded me down with playing cards previously held in reserve for my parents' long-past weekend bridge games (played until my mother took up gin), labored translations of Ibsen and Anatole France, my mother's *Boston Cooking School Cookbook* (eventually left alone and unconsulted on its shelf, as she had long since switched to frozen dinners); I was even given small boxes of coins with holes in their middles and whose weightlessness suggested their countries' precarious economies.

Waiting for us, if not for our cargo, was my wife, presenting an aspect alternating between empathy and shock. She was a dutiful daughter and so part of her saw a dutiful son followed by two other dutiful sons (who had only just begun, after their fifth trip, to complain about going, yet again, to Grandpa's). But her tolerance soon descended into dismay when the boys rushed in with what they called treasure (as I did also, secretly), objects velvet with dust, succeeded by rusty implements I promised to restore through the miracle of oil and steel wool.

In the hallway, though, she was confronted with the real thing, the furniture. What she saw there, and, worse, imagined was awaiting her at various covert staging areas, she was certain was about to invade *her* house (all vestiges of feminism would disappear at these moments). More clear-sighted than I, she knew that the carved claws at the end of the tapered legs of the Queen Anne chairs were there as more than period styling. These sentient decorations, she understood, had now uncompromisingly positioned themselves in our living room's foreground.

The question of accommodation, of course, went beyond the mere location of this or that item, and an aura of parental and generational mortality hovered over all these domestic objects. The presence of my grandfather's nail box led me to consider that at least some of the things appearing in our apartment belonged once to my father's father. Later, as I was about to hang one of my grandfather's paintings next to my side of the bed, I envisioned a hall of mirrors of both receding and successive generations of dutiful sons salvaging the possessions of aging or deceased fathers. These things, if not household gods after all, nevertheless had something of the status of relics.

Do we only awaken fully to others' dilemmas when they step across our own transoms? Is self-consciousness just a more finely extruded form of egotism? I began to notice how many of my friends had lately impounded in basements and storage vaults futons, Parsons tables, and tubular Breuer chairs of early—and childless—married days in order to defer to the graceful swells of Biedermeier and elderly, darkened shades of ornamented mahogany. Perhaps all that we were about to cast off was only the accumulated flotsam of single days. Now we were parents, too, and, like those before us, were finally in harness with all the trappings.

Some evenings, I would visit my father and his house in the empty darkness, without the protection of the boys. One night, I had made the familiar left turn onto his street and found the house missing, stolen. It had always been there, set atop a large keystone wedge of property that defined the arc in the street's perfectly symmetrical U. Suddenly, there was no house. Instead, there was the Siberian wasteland of 1906 (when my father was two years old) after the devastation of a monumental meteor impact, the craters of Passchendaele (when he is sixteen) lighted by flares. Most familiarly, I saw the science-fiction films of my black-and-white 1950s childhood—aliens had landed and had made off with the house, its goods, and my dad. This, then, was the ultimate move. And there I sat, hunched in the driver's seat, forehead pressed against the steering wheel, searching the car's instruments for orientation. The scene was, of course, only a momentary bit of theater caused by a neighbor's high intensity, burglar-riveting searchlights, ones activated most likely by a cat rather than by the legendary Fantomas. As the lights then went out, my father's house was put back. And I had been rehabilitated.

What had been glimpsed by me then was the heart's chasm, which had lately been revealing itself. It was a view I could not bear for long. In fact, seeing had begun to become a bit of a problem, as my retinas had begun to snap and flutter like the sails on a boat having trouble coming about. I had developed something that my ophthalmologist told me was "ocular migraine," where a perfect circle one morning had been inscribed on my field of vision. The doctor tried to allay my fear that I was beginning to lose my sight, as had been the case for my father years earlier and for whom the world was only getting murkier, and who was getting more and apprehensive about what he could less and less apprehend. One cause for such an "event" as mine, my doctor told me, was "stress," although "distress" would have come closer to the truth. Whatever I felt about either word, I was not particularly accomplished at easing my tense estate. Resist as I might, I became regularly afflicted by such random internal seizures. I had become a disappointment to years of costly, male, Republican, Episcopalian training.

The degree of upset that I was privately fostering was exactly what I think my father was trying to help my sister and me avoid. He was now trying to be a good father, which was also why we were in such a painful situation. For, in the selling of his house and planning for his move away, he had wanted to shield us from some of the pain of his eventual death. He wanted us to be "ready," as he perhaps was not, when he had taken lonely and un-remarked trips to his mother's tiny stucco house on Orloff Avenue in the Bronx after her delirious death in a hospital when she was in her nineties. At that earlier time, into our family home flowed the same familiar artifacts, many of which were now filling my own New York apartment.

In pulling up stakes when he did, my father wanted to spare my sister and myself such a double, really exponential, sense of loss. Even years before, he was stressing preparedness in anticipation of his mortality by having me sign powers of attorney, informing me of various life insurance policies, guiding me to stashes of important papers (copies of wills, codicils, cemetery deeds and maps), along with providing the location of keys to safety deposit boxes. For on his death I am to straight-arm Grief and Probate and make a dash for the bank.

Shaken twenty years ago by his own chronic eye problems, which subtly threw him off course, "When I die" for a while had become a familiar trope of an otherwise healthy man. Try as I might, I could not get such preemptive instructions right, for my otherwise impressive memory, one that I had inherited from him, failed me. Such mental lapses became the last pocket of resistance to the responsible fellow I had slowly become. Periodically, my father would plow the sea by reminding me of where everything of legal record was. I denied the need to remember. Look at how sound he was.

And while he was still relatively fit in his mid-eighties, a misplaced step flung him down the stairs and into the hospital. And he then knew, even when I didn't want to, that it was time to sell his house, time to move. And so we did. My sister, who is a realist, took all the furniture she could get and faithfully reassembled it in her emptied dining and living rooms, where the couch of my lost summer days re-established itself. To my father, her place looked like home. Looking on, I was left with tears for passing things.

III

It is his desire of sympathy that lies at the bottom of the great heap of his babblement. He wants to enrich all his enjoyments by steeping them in the heart of some friend. I do not think of him in danger of living so solitary a life as much as mine has been.

—Nathaniel Hawthorne, *Twenty Days with Julian & Little Bunny*

ACORNS

"First it must have meant a collection of acorns."
—Vico, *The New Science*

The last of them sounded at night, intruding on the faint beginnings of sleep. Dropping from the large white oak that shelters my house, the acorn smacked decisively into a third-floor eave, rolled onto the roof below and then off into the driveway to await its fate in the form of my radials. That morning's arterial current, set in motion by high crosswinds, had by evening become a random, slow drip. For much of the day I had been sitting on my porch, registering their descent as they cracked across roof tiles, chimed on gutters, and rasped across the louvers of the shutters the way a Cajun musician's knuckles flick over a washboard. They had been spreading a general clattering, nutty hail throughout the neighborhood. I listened to their progress, knowing we were literally being shelled. What I later in the evening took to be the last, solitary nut struck the house with the force of a cue ball being slapped onto a pool table. Taking its word as final, I rolled over and went to sleep.

Most of the acorns survived the daily arrivals and departures of our cars, and I retrieved a few to examine and instruct my sons in the wonders of gestation, gravity, growth of the abscision layer (which allows them to separate from the tree at the right moment), and chlorophyll loss, for no longer do these little nuts possess the glaucous green of August. Still, the little brown projectiles are as symmetrical and polished as if crafted by the most accomplished of wood-turners.

During my childhood, the acorns' scattered presence proclaimed the opening of school and the promise of fall. Afternoons, we would fashion them into elfin pipes, using my parents' bone-handled steak knives to prize off their caps, scoop out the meat of the nut and bore a hole large enough to receive their knobby oak twig stems. As they began to brown and crack in the later part of the season, acorns became shrunken heads and comic faces, beret over balding crown, attached to pipe cleaner bodies. The more experimental among us would attempt to taste their peculiar flesh. The nut, fuzzy and sectioned, once taken from its carapace was nibbled at, while others waited, expecting a panicked clutching of the throat and sudden, thrilling, cinematic death. Inevitably, though, acorns served the cause of war. Too young for slingshots and thus exempt from blindness-by-acorn, we threw them in great handfuls at imagined enemies. We never had to stockpile this ammunition, such was its abundance, and eventually squirrels and time would dispose of them all.

Then for decades, acorns ceased to be, along with other natural wonders of childhood in the fall—empty cicada skins, the larvae having oozed out their split backs; orange and black-banded woolly bear caterpillars; dogwood berries as red as our mothers' nail polish; leaves heaped into papery, flammable mattresses; and maple seeds turned into false noses, their sap a short-lived glue (with the more waggish of us making them peek out through pants zippers).

More likely, though, one October an active but solemn boy, once glad in nature, ceased to notice the oaks' fallen corn and began to live a more circumscribed life indoors, but one not necessarily more interior. The spaciousness and freedom of the outdoors were replaced by a floor-by-floor monitoring of his mother's secret and distracted passage through their old and large, cypress-shingled home. Perhaps that first boy, too, like the acorns, passed out of existence. There followed the troubled dreams of adolescence and a torpid awakening into adulthood, a time when an uncertain, partly-formed self emerged and moved hesitantly through the physical world.

The acorns were eventually called back into being, as were many lost things, by yet another small boy—my first son, Paul. Reminded of myself, I grew into becoming a father. Like David Copperfield, Paul was a magical boy, and all the lost treasures of childhood flooded once more into what had long been a well-defined, familiar vacuum. Rediscovered and recovered for him were my turret-lensed microscope, the slides I had stained, and all my Herbert Zim "Golden" nature books—insects, stars, flowers, and, especially, my beloved *Trees of North America*. One September, when he was about three and we were visiting Washington, D.C., we beheld a crowd of fallen acorns in astonishing abundance as we crossed north over the Capitol grounds. My dutiful son had professed an interest in Federal architecture, and we pointed ourselves toward the luminous white steps of the Supreme Court. We were stopped short, though, by the presence of acorns. Even the Capitol dome seemed to bear a resemblance, albeit a blanched one, to the tiny objects at our feet. In those bicameral environs we found representatives from both the black and white oak families. Official Washington held no further charms, as our pockets strained from collecting the elongated tapering acorns of the chestnut oak and those of the rounded overcup oak, whose clasping stem resembles a knit cap rudely pulled over the acorn's face—an acorn incognito.

On our return through the Northeast there were further discoveries of black jack and shingle oak acorns, their fattened sides bulging like a child's top. Back at home one Sunday we ascended into acorn heaven, laying out our gleanings on a thick-planked table.

This September, acorns fell in an atmosphere of remembrance. In the beginning, before I fell asleep one night, I heard their slow and weighty drip start as high up as sixty feet on the tree whose thickening bole is steadily encroaching on my driveway. The next morning, I informed Paul of their aggressive knocking, hoping that mention of them would be as evocative as the dipping of a madeleine. But he is now a loose-limbed, rangy teenager who favors Seattle-based grunge bands, Grateful Dead t-shirts that drape the knees, and high-top black sneakers with unkempt laces the color of old plaster. With a respectful but bemused blink he acknowledged my sense of wonder (this, after all, was the father who kept his family up through the greater part of a lunar eclipse). He said that he'd slept through it all. I then drove him to school and returned home to spend another morning alone, engrossed in what was becoming, in these autumn convections, a downpour of acorns.

There is a strategy in the steady pounding of this bombardment. As many another crouching civilian had learned before me, the night during which I believed the shelling had ended, it hadn't. Instead, the acorns' fall, sometimes punctuated by long silences, continued for more than a week after I thought it was going to stop. In fact, war raged on among the oaks, maples and a rare, ancient black walnut, each carpeting the area with fruit and seed seeking, as rapidly as possible, to burrow in, strangle the others' roots, and stunt competitors with their broad-leafed shade. The black walnut seemed to be firing blanks; its large green-vaulted nuts fell mainly on the driveway, where my younger son Gabriel and I collected them, staining our fingers light brown in pursuit of their thickly-guarded, tasty meat.

Meanwhile, the maples and oaks had captured terrain among my pachysandra and myrtle. If the winner is the one with the most marbles at the end of the game, the maples were clearly victorious. Nevertheless, despite the presence of hundreds of such saplings, and a few dozen nascent oaks, there remain on my property only three adult trees: a white oak, a Norway maple, and a black walnut, all old and very large. Over the past seventy years, they have been protected by the owners of the house, while their offspring have been systematically exterminated. For four or five years the eager saplings were allowed to push their covert way up to the very top of my six-foot-high hedge, becoming as prevalent as gray hairs caught in a brush. Finally, asserting my manorial rights, I came along and pulled them all out. The oaks posed a less visible threat, their main root growing off to the side rather than rapidly down and out like those of the maples, and they never attained a height of more than six or seven inches. If they had, I would have been as ruthless with them as I was with the maples, which I wrenched up root and branch (in the tradition of my Scottish ancestors, Stuarts and Culbertsons—atavistic terminators in kilts) and with whose dismembered fragments I filled innumerable trash bags. Feeling more, perhaps, like Emerson's "red slayer," I went to bed with my blood up. But the little oaks had simply stopped and gone no further. Aldo Leopold, on his sandy Wisconsin acres, noticed the same phenomenon and attributed the cause to the appetite of rabbits for the bark of the young oak. I could say rabbits, but there are none here; they were wiped out from the suburbs long ago by, I suspect, the ever-increasing cat population. I remember the same pattern of arrested growth occurring at my childhood home. There were three large oaks, many smaller flowering dogwoods, a sassafras, and a monstrous tulip tree. After reaching a certain point, all their saplings ceased to grow.

As a child, I loved all our trees—I even inventoried the dogwoods—but it was the high oaks that held me. In awe of their size, I wanted to climb all three, dreaming of riding their upper branches, conquering their summits, becoming airborne among their leaves. Selecting the largest, I hugged its rough and furrowed hide, stretching my arms as far as they would go, and pressed my cheek against the trunk. Fingers raking the bark, I inched my feet upward, but progressed only a few feet before my sneakers lost their grip and slipped back down. I kept this up until my cheek and the inside of my knees grew as flayed and red as Marsyas.

In all my attempts at childhood transcendence, I never seemed to realize that many large trees make ascent close to impossible; I would have had to go up at least forty feet before I encountered the first limb. Nevertheless, I was great with desire to be borne above my house, to be free of its darkened interiors. Like Calvino's young *illuministi* baron, Cosimo, who refuses to eat his dinner of snails, those night creatures of the ground. I wanted to defy my parents at the dining room table, fling open the window and leap into the trees. (His point of embarkation was a Holm oak.) I wanted Cosimo's ability not only to stay balanced among their branches, but also his resolve to create a realm there, an "ideal state in the trees," to traverse the leafy canopy from Italy to the rest of enlightened Europe, to live and love high up, to never come down. Like many another child, however, I remained earthbound at our mahogany table all my growing years, becoming more silent and retreating into the domestic woods that surrounded me.

In middle age, I am now again out of doors. I no longer feel the need to scramble up my oak, although I know that through Paul's third-floor window I could easily jump for a limb and swing out into its leaves. And then perhaps go on, like Cosimo, to the next limb, and the one after that. . . . Instead, I sit out on my porch, which is a bit like the deck of a ship and even seems to list slightly when I prop my feet against the railing. Sometimes I put down my book and walk to where the acorns are falling fastest.

When I'm not reading or daydreaming to acorns, I've been repairing some of the porch's broad and weathered steps. The spherical ornaments topping the two newel posts are also cracked and have to go. I have sanded, primed, and painted their replacements. I then pry off the originals and center the new ones, screwing them into the spongy wood, which eventually will have to be doweled. Paul helps me with one and Gabriel assists with the other. These replacements will be the first things visitors touch on coming to our house. They are shaped like acorns.

DOGWOODS

My youngest boy must see trees as parents, as he so thoughtlessly depends upon their limbs to be borne into the sky. From my angled view through the kitchen skylight, I watch him ascend some forty feet off the ground. He sees me, too, through a screen of leaves the dark-red of dried blood, and, once at the top, he playfully snaps off a withered branch. He wants to see if I will rise to the tumbling, crackling bait. But I am certain of him, I think, hoping the tree will not let him go, as the ground is varicose with exposed roots. Where he is, the upper branches are a mobile of yo-yos, failed toy parachutes, action figures tied to strings, offerings he has flung into the tree over the years.

Our dying dogwood, though, out in the front yard, is his favorite. Fronting our porch, where I am often perched in a chair, the tree hasn't the acute angles of the more ample maple in the back. Rather, its limbs shoot straight out like a gymnast's arms as he performs on the rings. These branches are low enough for the boy to boost himself up without the aid of the folding chair upon whose back he needs to get aboard the maple.

This dogwood is his republic of leaves where he carries up soccer balls, hoists up planks for jerrybuilt catwalks. His favorite aerie, though, is of the tree's fashioning. A flakey, bark-covered glove, four splayed branches cup him at the dogwood's not-so-high, high point. This is his reading room in the more hospitable seasons, and I can often spy him among the short-lived ivory brachts of spring, the bright green leaves of summer, ones later garnished by the red berries, the bright nail polish of a mother—perfect bloody droplets of the fall. Preferring the image of indolence to its reality, like Itard's wild boy, he executes a leap into the branches below. Many are quite supple, while others break off from their own weight. Gabriel is caught by a living one, and he then drops to the ground.

A single dogwood was part of my childhood, too. And it was also dying. I think this species has a life span like ours; it's shorter than the lofty, imperious hardwoods, and thus the dogwood, whose fallen petals curl forlornly on the earth below, is always in the embrace of a more noticeable mortality. When I was a boy, the oval scales that formed the outer layer of bark resembled the dark, dry, mossy patches on the backs of my grandfather's hands. The smallish tree took years dying, being slowly consumed from within, as was also true for him.

Like that tree of an earlier time, my tree here is giving up one branch at a time, withered and brittle at the tip, its sap turned back, gone somewhere else. The previous owners tried to stop this progress and lopped off one thick lower limb, leaving an untended stump.

Gabriel has now gone off, led elsewhere by his interests. He knows nothing of diseases of trees, this one is all invisible, and inevitably fatal, encroachments, or of those of adults, either, thinking that his grandfather, at 93, ran out of sap, got papery and brittle, slept, slept some more, and then slept all the time.

IV

only because I was asleep,
only because I was the soundbox
of their stories.

—Valerio Magrelli, *The Contagion of Matter*

"TASTE THIS" – A EULOGY

It seems perhaps only fitting that I should be told of my father's passing while returning examination books to my college class, those thin, blue booklets being one of the objects I associated most with my always-writing father when I was a child and my head came just about up to his pencil-enclosed hand. I remember vividly the red hieroglyphs he made across the pages of the exams of his Columbia University students, using pencils that had no erasers, suggesting that he never made a mistake. I sometimes half seriously believe that I became a college professor myself so that I might continue to secure an unending supply of such booklets, accompanied perhaps by the authority he seemed to invest in them. Using them in my classes will now more than ever be a memorializing gesture.

So it's a few of the little legacies of my father that I'd like to celebrate on this day. In fact, in attempting to put my thoughts down on paper, I first had to clear away all the piles of paper on the dining room table before I could make room for pen and pad. If you ever visited our house in Manhasset, you would know that Dad seemed to have a horror of bare work surfaces. And my sister, Jeanne, and I have surely followed suit in this quest to cover every available desk and tabletop at home and at work.

Quite a number of the papers that surrounded me as I wrote this include words, and even thoughts, of my own, and I'd like to acknowledge how much over the years my father shaped my idea of what a writer does. And that modest idea is that you should stay at your desk. That's the not-so-easy key to becoming a writer. In fact, just two days ago my college gave me an award for my own capacity for staying at my desk, the result of which has been quite a number of publications, ones almost always written with an image of my father in mind, pounding rhythmically at his monumental, black Remington, laughingly called a portable. A good portion of my award is his.

It's a more intangible but more enduring legacy of his, though, that I'd like to conclude with, and that was his buoyant joy at living and how that joy often informed his smallest acts. I remember best its pure communication twice. The first time was when I was about four, during a June evening in Manhasset, a time I much disliked as I had to go to bed while adults stayed up and the sun was still out. Before sleep set in, I'd observe the course of its declining rays as through the window they sectioned and washed the wallpaper yellow. I'd watch hazily as the tops of the oaks would go from green to green-brown, then brown-green; then the sun's rectangular shape on the wall would be gone, and I would be asleep. On one of those nights my father was barbecuing for friends and had promised, on kissing me goodnight, that he would bring me a surprise. And it wasn't long before he returned to my room bearing a well-charcoaled hot dog on a roll. Sitting on the edge of my bed, he offered me an already bitten end. "Taste this," he said. Perhaps nothing has ever again rivaled that magical bite, but what he gave me in that moment was a taste for the everlasting wonder in the smallest things and the most basic acts—giving, between a father and son.

He did something like this once more when I had become a father and I had brought Paul, then around three, out to his house for a regular Saturday visit. At the time, he could still walk about the house and so he sat on the front lawn, wearing one of his classic, splashy, flower-print Hawaiian shirts, while Paul, in his brass-buckled, red-corduroy Oshkoshes, ran giddy ellipses around him, and I photographed. Paul then stopped, looked into my father's eyes. A bright object suddenly flashed between them—a quarter, always a child's coin. Young and old, both were delighted. All three of us were. May we all have such bright memories. Thank you.

PEARS

Today I bought pears here in Wadena to begin my residence as a visiting writer. My host, Kent Sheer, had driven me to the Wadena True Value, where he had tried to entice me to buy "our" (a.k.a., Central Minnesota's) turkey and wild rice sausage, but I would have none of gizzards and grain. Instead, I headed off for the fruit section. Coming from a tree whose genus is *Pyrus communis*, a pear or two was what I, a new arrival, had to have. I don't know the many varieties of this fruit and can only conjure a few names: Anjou, Bartlett, Seckel; that's pretty much it. The three I bought were a speckled yellow brown, silting into a fading green, a muted blend that I hoped was carrying my pear closer toward ripeness.

I'm not a good judge of a pear's freshness; they're hardly as simple as apples, which if they're firm, you pick one up and bite in. The solidity and shape of pears, though, don't give them the lightness and evenly distributed weight of apples. Pears are compact and hard, hard as rocks, actually, dense and grave with specific gravity. I tried to pick up some that gave a bit of give, but this supposed tenderness was likely my imagination, for when I tentatively bit into one at home, it was . . . hard as rocks. I let the second selection sleep on its side undisturbed for two more days and then sliced into it the way my father did—part of his *politesse* with fruit, cutting, not biting. He'd bring me six even sections on a plate when I was a teen in the living room reading. This one was excellent.

My dad loved a bit of fruit, savored the juices, the entire activity of preparing, serving, and eating, offices hinting at the sensuousness behind his solid, upstanding Republican affect, one fundamentally jolly and good-natured, and which I seem to have largely inherited, along with a jigger's worth of my mother's madness. Pears, cherries, red grapes, and peaches, the runny fruits were his favorites; and was it this physicality my mother desired to avoid by going to bed later than he? Perhaps the juniper in gin may be considered fruit, for, as Spenser tells us, "Sweet is the Iunipere." My mother would stay on in the living room reading, as my father headed upstairs, his hand lightly gracing the polished mahogany banister. Certainly I possess his taste-in-touch.

When he was in his seventies and living alone in too large a house, I would bring him cherries, Bings, and I would always laugh at his standing joke about Crosby not fitting into the bag. And when we would shop together, he would buy pears, which he could hardly see but knew well by hand through his delicate, tapering papery fingers.

I buy a few pears whenever I'm away somewhere writing, like now, where my studio is in the town's assisted-living center, The Pines, and which is filled with a number of widowers like my dad once was. I have a shyness about buying them and linger before their open baskets, never quite able to remember what I succeeded with last time. Since I like both the idea of pearness and something of the thing itself, too, I just choose a color, usually red or yellow, the color of maple leaves in the fall. I handle each one carefully, though I learn little from doing this. Each day here, I'll check them with my right hand, which directs my most responsive fingers, and gently test the taut middle, one pear always lost in the trial for ripeness. The second is usually perfection a day or two later, desire finally grafted onto the fullness of the fruit. Its swelling side makes way for my father's penknife, his still-sharp blade easing through the slightly grainy flesh, making thin, even slices, leaving a square core behind. I eat those gleaming pieces slowly, wetting my fingers.

At home, my wife Leslie, who wants to give me all things, will sometimes buy me pears knowing that they mean something—what some people, perhaps the French, like to call the presence of absence. Knowing the nurturing lore of her grandparents' Maryland farm, she puts them in a paper bag, sure that this is how they will ripen. And they do.

LAST WORDS

"Reamy, Don't dawdle."

"I should write a book."

WORKS QUOTED:

Adams, Ansel. *The Negative, Exposure, Development.* Hastings on Hudson: Morgan & Morgan, 1971.

Duras, Marguerite. *Reading.* Tr. Mark Polizzotti. Cambridge, Mass.: Lumen Editions, 1998.

Frost, Robert. *The Poetry of Robert Frost*, ed. Edward Connery Lathem. New York: Henry Holt & Co., 1969.

Hammerstein, Oscar and Richard Rodgers. R & H Concert Library.

Hawthorne, Nathaniel. *Twenty Days with Julian & Little Bunny by Papa.* New York: New York Review Books, 2003.

Locke, John. *Educational Writings of John Locke*, ed. James L. Axtell. London: Cambridge University Press, 1969.

Magrelli, Valerio. *The Contagion of Matter.* Tr. Anthony Molino. New York: Holmes & Meier Publishers, 2000.

Frame, Donald. *Montaigne: A Biography.* New York: Harcourt, Brace & World, 1965.

Milosz, Czeslaw. *Milosz's ABC's.* Tr. Madeline G. Levine. Farrar, Straus & Giroux, 2001.

Spenser, Edmund. *Spenser's Minor Poems.* Ed. by Ernest De Selincourt. Oxford: Clarendon Press, 1910.

Vico, Giambattista. *The New Science.* Tr. Thomas Bergin and Max Fisch. Ithaca, NY: Cornell University Press, 1958.

REAMY JANSEN is Professor of English and Humanities at Rockland Community College (SUNY) and Adjunct Professor of Media Studies at Fordham University's College at Lincoln Center.

His poetry and prose have been published in a wide variety of literature magazines such as *The International Review, Alimentum, The Literature of Food, Gargoyle, Evansville Review, Oasis,* and many others. He has held residencies at Yaddo, Gell House, the Virginia Center for Creative Arts, NY Mills Arts and Cultural Retreat, and the Oberfeltzer Kunstlerhaus in Germany. His awards include the SUNY Chancellor's Award for Creativity and Scholarship, Mellon Fellowship, New Millennium Writing, Talking Rivers Review, Geraldine R. Dodge fellowships; he has also received eight Pushcart nominations.

He is Contributing Editor to *The Bloomsbury Review of Books* and Editor of its short prose section, "The Out of Bounds Essay." He is Editor of Creative Nonfiction for *Hamilton Stone Review.*

Breinigsville, PA USA
08 April 2010
235699BV00001B/3/P

GREECE AND THE
BRITISH CONNECTION
1935–1941

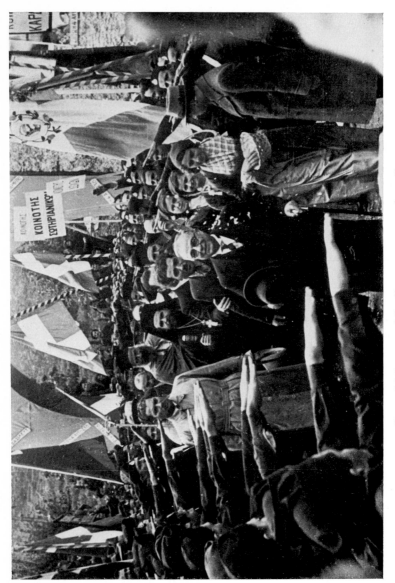

General Metaxas, while dictator, at a popular rally

Greece and the
British Connection
1935–1941

JOHN S. KOLIOPOULOS

OXFORD
AT THE CLARENDON PRESS
1977

Oxford University Press, Walton Street, Oxford OX2 6DP

OXFORD LONDON GLASGOW
NEW YORK TORONTO MELBOURNE WELLINGTON
IBADAN NAIROBI DAR ES SALAAM LUSAKA CAPE TOWN
KUALA LUMPUR SINGAPORE JAKARTA HONG KONG TOKYO
DELHI BOMBAY CALCUTTA MADRAS KARACHI

British Library Cataloguing in Publication Data
Koliopoulos, John S.
  Greece and the British connection, 1935–1941
  1. Greece, Modern – Foreign relations – Great Britain
  2. Great Britain – Foreign relations – Greece, Modern
  I. Title
  327.495'041   DF787.G7
  ISBN 0–19–822523 7

*Printed in Great Britain
at the University Press, Oxford
by Vivian Ridler
Printer to the University*